BEATEN PATHS
ARE SAFEST

From D-Day to the Ardennes
Memories of the 61st Reconnaissance Regiment
50th (TT) Northumbrian Division

To Margaret & Derek
from Aunt Edna
X X

Dedication:

To all who served with the

RECONNAISSANCE CORPS

(The Royal Armoured Corps)

During the War of 1939 – 1945
Especially to the memory of those comrades
Killed in action or mortally wounded

O VALIANT HEARTS

BEATEN PATHS
ARE SAFEST

From D-Day to the Ardennes
Memories of the 61st Reconnaissance Regiment
50th (TT) Northumbrian Division

Compiled by

Roy Howard (A Sqdn.)

BREWIN BOOKS

First published by
Brewin Books Ltd, 56 Alcester Road,
Studley, Warwickshire B80 7LG in 2004
www.brewinbooks.com

ISBN 1 85858 256 3

A Cataloguing in Publication Record
for this title is available from the British Library.

Typeset in Times
Printed in Great Britain by
The Cromwell Press

CONTENTS

THE 61ST RECONNAISSANCE REGIMENT

The Reconnaissance Corps was formed in 1941 and trained alongside other newly formed UK Special Forces – Commando's, SBS, SAS and Parachute Regiments.

The story of 61st RECONNAISSANCE REGIMENT is probably the least recorded of all the Recce Regiments but surely must be one of the most distinguished. Having led the invasion of Europe on D.Day 6th of June 1944, 61st Recce were in continuous active operations mainly with the 50th Northumbrian (TT) Division, but was called upon to work with No 47 Marine Commando, 8th Armoured Brigade, 11th Armoured Division, and due to the disaster which befell the Recce Rgt. of the 43rd West Riding Division when that unit struck a mine off the Normandy beaches and was destroyed, the 61st took their place until they could be made back up to strength.

In Holland during the 'MARKET GARDEN' operation they were again with the 50th (TT) Div. Protecting the left flank of the Guards Armoured Division as far as the town of Grave, and then with the U.S. 101st Airborne Div.

In the Ardennes campaign, the 50th (TT) Division had been disbanded, and the 61st Recce operated initially with 11th Armoured Div. Then with the U.S. 101st & 82nd Airborne Divisions – The Independent Belgian Brigade, and finally as an Independent Recce Regiment.

The book entitled "THIS BAND OF BROTHERS" by Jeremy Taylor (1947) records the history of THE RECONNAISSANCE CORPS long before Stephen E. Ambrose (1992) used this title for the Epic story of the U.S. 101st Airborne Division (Easy Company).

We few, we happy few, we band of brothers,
For he today that sheds his blood for us
Shall be my brother; be he ne'er so vile,
This day shall gentle his condition;
And gentlemen in England, now a-bed,
Shall think themselves accurs'd, they were not here,
And hold their manhood cheap, whiles any speaks
That fought with us upon St Crispin's day.

(William Shakespeare)

FOREWORD

Ernest Roy Howard was born on September 12th 1921, second son of Robert Ernest and Louisa May Howard of Sutton Coldfield, West Midlands. Educated at Bishop Vesey Boys Grammar School Sutton Coldfield, he served with the army cadets as a schoolboy.
Volunteered to join up on 20th October 1939 aged 18.

Enlisted into the Royal Warwickshire Regiment Embodied Territorial Army and was posted to 9th Battalion.

Sent to France with the British Expeditionary Force (B.E.F.) and was evacuated from the beaches of Dunkirk.

November 4th 1941 transferred to the Reconnaissance Corps and posted to 61st Battalion.

Served with 61st Reconnaissance Regiment Royal Armoured Corps 50th Northumbrian Division.

1st January 1944, granted rank of War Substantive Corporal, promoted in the field to acting Sergeant later posted 16th May 1945 to 61st Training Regiment Royal Armoured Corps as acting Captain. Released to Royal Army Reserve on 14th March 1946.

Married Edna Mary Chatwin April 3rd 1947.

Held in Army Reserve until discharged on 30th June 1959.

Roy Howard served with the 61st Recce from its beginning. Like so many Veterans, he kept his war experiences locked up in his memory, rarely revealing his part in the events that shape the world today.

1937 (School Cadet Bishop Vesey's School) *1939 (Royal Warwickshire Regiment)* *1944 (Reconnaissance Corps)*

It was not until much later in his life, after his first return visit to Normandy in 1989 stirred him up, that he felt able to share some of those experiences with his family, along with the realisation that very little written history *(official or otherwise)* actually existed of the 61st Reconnaissance Regiment.

Theirs was no small part. Instrumental in some of the most decisive and desperate actions in the north-western European campaigns of World War Two. After discovering that the greater part of the War Diary for the 61st Recce was 'missing', he set about compiling his own record from many sources including personal memories that had taken him and the rest of his generation of young men to their limits.

Sadly Roy suffered a severe stroke in 1992 and was unable to complete this work. Passing away in 1996 a much-loved husband, father of three, and a great friend.

This is an attempt to re-produce, to the best of my limited abilities, *his* work.

Intended to honour the memory of the great efforts made by his comrades of the 61st Reconnaissance Regiment, and for the information of future generations. 'Lest we forget'- I hope he would have approved.

His 'Band of Brothers' are the young men who fell along the way.

Mark Howard

Every effort has been made to trace and acknowledge ownership of copyright material appearing in this book. Any further information on sources would be welcomed and should be addressed to Mark Howard c/o the publishers.

ACKNOWLEDGEMENTS

Bayeux War Museum   -   Curator.
BBC History web site   -   Peoples War*
Bovington Tank Museum   -   Curator.
Brewer, Family   -   Derek Brewer*
Commonwealth War Graves Commission. -   John Gimblett.
Dawson, Family   -   Wilf, Vera & John (OCA)
Gateway to Victory   -   Tallandier.
Imperial War Museum   -   Roderick Suaby.
Military Affairs   -   Editor.
Newspapers   -   London Gazette, Sunday Pictorial.
Old Comrades Association   -   News Letters.
Public Records Office
September '44   -   De Haan.
Victory in Normandy   -   Belchem.

Subsequent additions*

Originally compiled by – Roy Howard. July 1991.

Ernest Roy Howard – 1921 -1996

INTRODUCTION

The information contained herein relates in particular to the brief history of the 61st Regiment, Reconnaissance Corps of the 50th Northumbrian (T.T.) Division which led the Invasion of Europe on the 6th June 1944.

Information and photos – with acknowledgement for extracts from the following Authorities:-

The Imperial War Museum
T.T. 41 Old Comrades Association Newsletter
'The Sharp End of War' by John Ellis
'Victory in Normandy' by Major General David Belchem
'This Band of Brothers' by Jeremy Taylor
'Operation Market Garden' by A K Altes, K Magry, G Thurimg, R Voskuil, De Haan
'Echoes over 30 years of war' by Major Frank Harding
'Sunday Pictorial' – September 1942 – BBC Radio Newscast
'Military Affairs' No 28 – 22nd January 1945
'Tomorrow's World at Large' – BBC 1 – TV
The London Gazette – 1941
'Caen – Anvil of Victory' by Alexander McKee

'Break-Out From Normandy Bridgehead. June 7th - 12th 1944' - Brigadier HJB Cracroft.

BBC History website. - My Bit: From Richmond, Yorkshire, To Europe – Don Aiken

With the passing of so many veterans, every effort to acknowledge their contributions is intended. Apologies to the families of those whom it has not been possible to contact. 'We will remember them!'

Lull'd in the countless chambers of the brain,
Our thoughts are linked by many a hidden chain;
Awake but one, and lo what myriads arise,
Each stamps its image as the other flies

Government Warning! - *A little salt may be added in places, but do not overuse*

GENERAL SIR BERNARD C.T. PAGET

General Sir Bernard C.T. Paget, K.C.B., D.S.O., M.C., prime architect in 1940 and 1941 of Britain's new armies and Colonel – Commandant of the Reconnaissance Corps.

THE RECONNAISSANCE CORPS

The Corp's stated duty was to "gather vital tactical information in battle for infantry divisions." Using armoured cars, universal carriers and trucks it was to scout enemy territory and then send the gathered information back using wireless radio. It was said of its men that ....

"Those who served [in the Recce Corps] had to be intelligent, enterprising, brave, enduring, and highly skilled." - Sir Arthur Brant.

About this time, an unofficial motto, which stayed with the Recce Corps throughout the war, was coined: -

Only the Enemy in Front .... Every Other Beggar Behind!
(Later used for the title of a book on The 'Recce' Corps by Richard Doherty)

Men of Reconnaissance regiments were also permitted to wear arm-of-service strips of green and yellow, - the colours of the Corps.

On 23 April 1941 a decision was reached on an official unit logo. The design, which finally became the Reconnaissance Corps badge, was the work of Trooper George Jones of 56 Recce. The badge consisted of a spearhead flanked by two bolts of lightning and incorporated a scroll, which read Reconnaissance Corps.

Two official mottoes were also adopted at this time. They were:

Ab Uno Disce Omnes - "From One Learn All", and
Via Trita, Via Tuta, - "Beaten Paths Are Safest".

A Recce Regiment consisted of 3 squadrons of Recce Troops, plus 1 Squadron in which was the Supply and Administration Sections. In addition it had a Signal Troop, Mortar Troop and an Anti-Tank Troop.

Regimental HQ was the nerve centre which controlled the Regiment when it was in action and which was in touch with higher formations i.e. Brigade or Division.
Each Recce Squadron consisted of 3 Scout Troops and an Assault Troop. Scout Troops being in Armoured Cars and Bren Carriers.

THE TEST

(Newsletter Old Comrades Association)

Sir William Mount's influence on the development of the Regiment was tremendous, always thinking of, improving equipment, and as reported in Newsletter No.6, 1971, he invented a system of mortar firing from the map, enabling direct mortar fire often to hit the target with the first round. Sgt. "Posh" Price now recalls the Test by which Sir William had to prove his point and the value of the innovation to his brains. In the Sergeant's own words: Sir William told me overnight to be ready with the Mortar Troop for a live bomb demonstration to very VIPs the next morning. Sir William was cock-a-hoop that it was to take place to prove to the 'Scrambled Egg Blokes' the wonderful accuracy developed by his system.

The big moment – Sir William rolling away with the Nobs, with the Mortars a mile behind awaiting orders over the radio. After half an hour - 'Action Imminent' – followed by 'Action', giving enemy position, map reference etc. Before you could say that a pedestrian is a man with a wife, two sons, three daughters and one car, the Mortars were on the ground and 'Key Mortar Ready' signalled, the other five Mortars laid onto the 'Key Mortars'.

Two shakes of a monkey's tail and the order to fire received – first bomb away. Waited the twenty-one seconds for the strike on target, ready for any corrections, i.e. Northings, Eastings or whatever sent back. The correction came quickly, I remember it well – 'Northeast five zero'. All mortars given the range and deflection quickly, and acknowledged promptly, when 'all mortars ready to fire' I signalled. 'Ten rounds rapid' came the order and sixty lovely ten-pound bombs flew to their unknown destination. One minute elapsed and back came the order, 'Target eliminated', stay where you are, we are coming back to you', and before you realised that a cynic is one who knows everything but believes nothing, a jubilant Sir William and a puzzled retinue of Top Brass arrived, wanting to know what had happened at the Mortar end on receipt of the first and subsequent orders.

Showing them Colonel Mount's chart and explaining the corrections for the conversion of the orders, I received a rather blank stare.

'Would I be good enough to explain again?' I did so, but the VIP shook his head in I'm sure utter disbelief, he obviously could not understand the system. In reply to pertinent questions (Me boss cat now) the VIP had to admit that the target he himself had selected just did not exist anymore. He then added a classical remark, 'Well Sergeant, we are supposed to be the Brains, but it's a bit beyond me and I thank you'. We grew six inches in stature and all finished in true Perry Mason style. Ha! Ha! Ha!

NCO's, responsible for laying Mortars plus range deflections, were Sergeant Rutter, Sergeant Ormerod and Corporal Cowley and of course, yours truly, Sergeant Price, who concludes his epistle that they were darned good chaps to have under any conditions, as Jerry was soon to find out when the system was used in earnest. And the Mortar crews themselves were excellent – always on the ball.

Sir William lies modestly low – so mud in your eye for shooting the line - Ed:

TT41 *(It's a great journey to life's end).*

TOUGH AS COMMANDOES –
NEW…SHOCK TROOPS - EYES OF THE ARMY….

'Dare-devil Cavalry' on mounts of steel – Men who Fall on the Enemy from the Skies- were headlines following the brief announcement in the London Gazette early '41 revealing the secret of Britain's latest military development – The Reconnaissance Corps. As tough as commandos, the men are being welded into shape at a Scottish training centre. Every man is a specialist. He may know all about wireless, the mainstay of reconnaissance; how to drive anything; how to find his way about strange country; how to clear minefields; how to hit both men and planes from the revolving turret of an armoured car – or he may be an assault trooper… But every member of the unit should also be able to take over the duties of another. Parachute troops similarly equipped are also formed. The main object of the Recce Corps is to find out what lies ahead of the advancing forces and to send back information. Officers and NCO's in charge of the most advanced units have to be able to get messages back at once and to receive others. They are the successors of the Scouts of the Boer War and the Cavalry of the last war….Each battalion - one to each infantry division has high speed cars, Bren Carriers, troop carrying trucks and motorcycles. It has anti-tank artillery, 55 rifles and grenades, batteries of mortars and hosts of Tommy-guns and light machine guns. One company produces crews for armoured cars and carriers. Another company produces signallers, mechanics and motorcyclists.

So from 1941 to March 1944 when we read that 172 men of the 1st Recce Regiment held two miles of the Anzio beach-head perimeter during the Germans first heavy counter attacks. They held at least two battalions - odds of ten to one and by aggressive night patrolling caused havoc and confusion in the enemy camp….. Such are extracts from the newspapers of the day….. and with a Roll of Honour of nearly 2500 Officers and other Ranks killed in action, 24 awarded the DSO, 148 the Military Cross, and 189 Military Medals, can only go to prove that the Recce reached its highest standard…….

THIS WAS US!
THE FIRST THRILLING STORY OF BRITAIN'S
'RECCIES' OUR SECRET ARMY IS READY

(With kind acknowledgements to THE SUNDAY PICTORIAL – SEPTEMBER 1942)

These men, every one picked for brain as well as brawn, will be the spearhead of our new-style army.

Inside the swinging gun-turret of a fast-moving armoured car I saw war streaming over the quiet soil of Kent. An army was on the move....

The squat dun-coloured armoured cars thundered on at 50mph. Behind them, Bren-gun carriers, lorry-drawn anti-tank guns and motorcycles, bunched like a closed fist, shot across the open heath. The weapons were old – the standard armament of an infantry division – but the tactics were new. Here was war from a new slant, for never in this history of modern warfare had men dared to fight like this. It was warfare moving across the countryside at the speed of an express train: something the Germans have not yet met. One day they will feel the real terror of it, for the army I saw moving across that stretch of heath is the secret army: it has not yet been in action. They call them the Reconnaissance Corps – the 'Reccies' for short. The men of the Reconnaissance Corps have taken on one of the toughest jobs of the war – the spearhead of our attack on Germany. They are elusive as guerrillas, fast as scouts, tough as commandos. At the moment you do not hear much about the men of the Reconnaissance Corps. Their moment in history has not yet come.

Behind this veil of secrecy Britain is building an army within an army; a secret force, complete in itself, which can be catapulted from the main body of the army, deep into the heart of enemy territory. An army which will roam behind enemy lines, spying, killing, sabotaging. And every moment of the day or night they will be in wireless communication with their divisional commander. Every move the enemy makes the 'Reccies' will note and transmit back to headquarters. That is their job, to spy on the enemy at close quarters. But with this difference. Every scrap of information they get will be fought for. They will snatch secrets from the Germans at the point of a blazing Bren-Gun.

Who are these 'Reccies'? As we rattled over wild scrubland in bone-shaking Bren-Gun carriers, bumped along winding cart tracks in armoured cars, I came to understand the kind of men they are. We reached a small river. The water was slimy and still, there was no bridge across but the river had to be crossed. "How deep is that?" barked the Colonel. A man's body whizzed past my ear, and a soldier fully equipped was floundering in mid-stream, trying to touch bottom, but his equipment held him up. "I'll go sir!" flashed a major. And before the Colonel had finished his nod of agreement, the major had dived in. He came up spluttering. "About eight feet sir." Before he had reached the shore a huge trooper was swimming across with a rope, one end of which was already tied to a tree stump. This trooper dug his heels into the ground on the opposite side and held the rope taut while the others pulled themselves across by it, hand over hand. One man dropped his Tommy Gun into the water; down he went after it and was under water so long I thought he would drown.

But he came up again, coughing mud and slime, Tommy Gun firmly grasped. In another two minutes, by means I must not disclose, the Bren-carriers were across and we careered forward.

The carriers had orders to attack a certain point. Over the wild rock-strewn heath they flew. One swerved suddenly and another crashed into it. The swerving one overturned, both scudded to a stop. 'My God, they are killed!' I heard myself shouting, and felt a sudden indignation that Bill Turner who happened to be close to them, was calmly taking photographs instead of running to help. But when I reached them the men – three men to a carrier – had already got out their Bren-Guns and were lying on the ground firing at their objective. None was killed and, though some may have been injured, they never disclosed the fact.

After the exercise the men talked about themselves, their peacetime jobs, their aspirations and their ideas on how the war should be fought. No two men had the same story. In civilian life some had been civil servants, farmers, shopkeepers, cavalry regiments. Yet certain things these young men had in common. They were all intelligent men. Most of them had brains enough to direct this war from a desk in Whitehall, but they had not wanted to see the war the easy way. They were men in search of adventure. They gloried in the physical hardships of their training. They made time their enemy, knocking seconds off every operation. During the last three years I have seen thousands of men undergoing infantry training. I know just how good our soldiers are, but in the 'Reccies' I saw something new. Every operation was streamlined. To cross barbed wire a man flung himself on the wire while other 'Reccies' used him as a doormat. To test a 'Reccies' initiative and split second decision he is sent out on a 'Blitz range' and attacked from all points. As the attackers close in on him he must fire from the hip. The words 'trapped', 'encircled', 'obstacles' are unknown to them. They do not wait for engineers to build them bridges across rivers. They have not time to wait for ladders to scale buildings. Everything is improvised, time reducing, hazardous. Here in the peaceful countryside of England I have seen them being taught the art of this new form of killing. Each man in the 'Reccies' is a specialist. He can operate almost any sort of army wireless equipment, can drive a Bren-Gun carrier, armoured car, three-ton lorry, can lay mines and help to clear mine-fields. He can fire every weapon the regiment carries. He is an expert.

Now the period of training and waiting is drawing to a close. Soon they will be teaching the Germans the final lessons of war on the plains of Europe. That is the moment every trooper in the Reconnaissance is waiting for.

His finger is on the trigger..........

SMILE FOR THE CAMERA

The Irish are now in the space race to land a man on the SUN.
The Americans say this is impossible, but the Irish say no, their man will land at night!

61ST RECCE. REGT:
ON TRAINING EXERCISES.
EXERCISE 'ORWELL'
(8TH – 10TH MAY 1943)

1. Humber Heavy Armoured Car. Light Recce. Car with Rev. J.L. Head. Chaplin to the Regiment. 2. 'A' Squadron Commander Major Brownrigg (later Colonel). 3. Lt. Col. Sir William Mount T.D. directing operations from his Light Recce. Car. 4. Man - handling a 6-pounder gun during the exercise (Anti-tank Troop).

5. *Firing a 6-pounder gun.* 6. *A 'Don R' takes cover behind his motor cycle.* 7. *A light armoured Recce. Car crossing difficult country.* 8. *A dismounted Bren gun in action.* 9. *61 Recce. 'A' Squadron, Roy Howard (5th from right, circled)*

THE REGIMENT'S MASCOT 'FOX' -
BY ERNIE BROBBIN 'A' SQDN.

(Newsletter Old Comrades Association)

Ernie Brobbin gave the following account of the Regiment's unique mascot to the Southern Daily Echo – Southampton 26/03/1994.

The original picture showing the fox on a lead with Capt. Compton Bishop was painted by Sandy Handley (B Sqdn) who sent copies as Christmas cards to a few members.

"Our Regiment had a unique mascot – a fox which our Troop Officer kept in his armoured car and took for walks!

It all began in January 1944 when we set up camp in Nightingales Woods, which today forms part of Romsey Golf course. We made our beds out of saplings – real Boy Scout stuff.

The time was spent waterproofing the engines. We were the most highly mechanised of any Army unit, with one vehicle per three men, which entailed a lot of motors being treated and tested for us drivers/mechanics.

One particular morning as dawn was breaking, another chap [*believed to be Roy Howard*] and I were on motor transport guard when we heard a 'baby' crying and went to investigate.

The 'baby' turned out to be an abandoned fox cub. The poor thing was crying after it had been left on its own.

Neither of us had come across a fox before, as we came from mining areas. We picked it up, took it back to camp, fed it on milk, and then made it a cage from saplings.

The cub prospered and eventually we decided to take it with us as a troop mascot.

Our Troop Officer, Captain Compton Bishop adopted it and kept it in his armoured car. After we reached Normandy, he would take it for walks at night on a lead!

We kept the fox until we got chased down the Ardennes in January/February the following year to help the Yanks out of the Battle of the Bulge.

It was the last time I saw the Captain or the fox. We were brought back to Belgium and the Regiment was broken up.

The Captain came from 17/21 Lancers and for many years I always wondered what happened to the pair of them.

Remarkably, by pure chance some eight years ago, I discovered that the Captain had survived the war and was still alive, but I still don't know what happened to the fox."

Ernie Brobbin 'A' Sqdn.

CHRONOLOGY OF EVENTS AND MOVEMENTS OF 61ST RECCE

June 6th	D-Day Landing on 'Gold Beach'
June 7th	Break out to Tessel Bretville
June 9th	Recce Jerusalem
June 10th	Tilly-Sur-Seulles
June 13th	Villers-Bocage
June 28th	Mondrainville (cross river Odon, west of Caen)
July 16th	Hottot-les-Bagues & Evrecy
July 30th	Caumont
August 1st	Return to Villers-Bocage (finally taken on August 4th)
August 12th	Briquessard (trench warfare)
August 25th	Vernon & hold Seine crossing
August 30th	Beauvais
September 1st	Arras
September 3rd	Tournai
September 4th	Lille
September 6th	Ghent/Courtrai
September 7th	Gheel (cross Albert canal)
September 11th	Burg Leopold (cross Meuse-Escault canal)
September 17th	Advance on left flank of 30 Corps to Mol & Valkenswald
September 18th	Hasselt & Eindhoven (link up with US 101st Airborne) at Veghel
September 19th	Grave (link up with US 82nd Airborne)
September 20th	Cross Nimegan Bridge over river Waal
September 22nd	Elst
September 24th	South bank of Rhine (West of Arnhem) Continuous patrols on 'Island' until 17th October
October 17th	Venray
October 18th	Aachen
October 20th	Iseghem (withdraw to disband)
December 16th	Reform & move to Namur
December 17th	Dinant
December 21st	Hotton & St Hubert
December 27th	Celles
December 30th	Houffalaize
December 31st	Rochefort
January 7th	Laroche
January 11th	Ourthe
January 22nd	St Joost (Nr Sittard)
January 25th	Return to Iseghem & disband.

A VETERAN'S PLEA -

When my long, slow journey's done
Will someone bear in mind
My whim to have a horsedrawn hearse
And not the motor kind
They cannot all be mechanised
There must be one survivor
To bear my bones within
And my ghost beside the driver

(From a 77 year old First World War
survivor of the Worcester Yeomanry)

A RECONNAISSANCE REGIMENT IN THE B.L.A.

By Lieutenant – Colonel P.H.A. Brownrigg D.S.O.

To C.O., 61st RECCE REGT. - Will you tell your Officers and men how grateful I am for all the grand work they have done? They have been simply magnificent, and although their battle history is not long as time goes it has been a glorious one, and every one of you can feel justifiably proud of all you have achieved. When much that has happened in the war is forgotten, the memory of your deeds will remain. My heart felt thanks to you one and all.

(Extract from a letter from MAJOR GENERAL D.A.H. GRAHAM. C.B.,C.B.E.,D.S.O., M.C.)

The whole history of the Reconnaissance Corps is short, lasting only about six years; and while the battle history of the 61st Reconnaissance Regiment is shorter than that of many others, its career is typical, I think, of the Corps. Our regiment began in 1941 with the appointment of the Commanding Officer Lieutenant-Colonel Sir William Mount, Bt.T.D., who was then a battery commander in the Berkshire Yeomanry; a Quartermaster from the Loyal Regiment, then in Singapore; an Adjutant from the Royal Berkshire Regiment; and an R.S.M. from the Seaforth Highlanders. To them were added drafts from the nine infantry battalions of the 61st Division; and soon afterwards further drafts from some ten other regiments from all over England. Many of the officers and men had naturally not wanted to leave their old units, so that at first their loyalties remained with the regiments whose buttons they still wore. There was much weeding out of the unfit and undesirable in the first few months.

Our equipment was equally diverse. Our alleged armoured cars were called Beaverettes. They had been made in a hurry for the expected Battle of Britain by adding thin armour plate to a civilian 10 - hp chassis. They were very tired by the time they came to us.

All this made for short tempers and long faces, silence in the mess and stern words from the orderly room. Once when the Transport Officer complained to the usually equable Adjutant that he hadn't received an important message he was sharply told; 'When I send you a message it's your duty to see that it reaches you.' But, thanks to the Commanding Officer, the transition from a conglomeration of mutually hostile drafts to a united regiment was quickly achieved. Our morale and equipment improved steadily until 1943, when the 61st Division was relegated to Home Forces, and we had to draft many of our best men away.

At this moment we had a wonderful stroke of luck (or shrewd manoeuvre by the Commanding Officer.) The 50th (Northumbrian) Division was back in England for the Normandy invasion, and had no reconnaissance regiment. After the Commanding Officer had made a number of swift trips to London we found ourselves chosen to fill the vacancy. So in January 1944, we motored from our coast-guarding duties in Kent to join our new division in Norfolk.

Only those who have experienced it can know the inferiority an unblooded regiment feels when surrounded by battle-scarred heroes. But the 50th Division made us so welcome, and refrained so carefully from flinging their blood and sand into our eyes, that we soon felt at home in what must have been the happiest of divisions in spite of all its casualties. The informal efficiency of the Divisional Headquarters was superb. During the Normandy campaign our Intelligence Sergeant went one day instead of the Intelligence Officer to get the latest 'picture' from Divisional Headquarters. As he was walking over to the Intelligence Map the Divisional Commander saw his black beret from his caravan, and called out, 'Hello Recce! What do you want!' When he was told he said, 'Come in here, I'll show you what's happening. They don't know anything over there.' Was it any wonder that General Graham's visits to the regiment were always immensely popular?

Our task for the invasion was twofold: First, to provide contact patrols with the assaulting battalions, working back to a control set at Divisional Headquarters; and, second, to land a skeleton reconnaissance regiment. This meant reorganising the Regiment. "C" Squadron found the contact patrols and some carriers with their crews to act as ammunition ferriers for 47 Marine Commandos at Port-en-Bessin. The assault reconnaissance regiment consisted of "A" And "B" Squadrons and Regimental Headquarters, all at about 40% of their full strength. The remainder of the Regiment was scheduled to land within the first month. For our special task we were allowed to chose much of our equipment, and so acquired a great number of half tracks, which were useful throughout the campaign, and lots of bicycles, which their owners thankfully discarded after three weeks of painful pedalling.

First vehicles ashore on D-Day were the light Recce Cars of Major Cave (C.Sqdn.) and his crew and that of Cpl. Howard and his crew (A.Sqdn.). Due to embarkation problems in the U.K. and the vagaries of war, they arrived on different landing craft and at opposite ends of the landing beach, but managed to rendezvous safely in the area inland beyond the dunes, and were able to radio beach information and R.V. positions to the C.O. and remainder of the landing force still aboard their landing craft.

Nearly half the contact patrols with the assaulting infantry were killed or wounded on D-Day, either on the beaches or before reaching them. Nevertheless, they justified themselves by getting much information back to Divisional Headquarters before it arrived by the normal channels and some of the patrols, whose sets had been shot-up, did great work with their weapons.

The plan for the skeleton regiment was to land from H plus 4 onwards, and concentrate with a composite force consisting of the 8th Armoured Brigade, an infantry battalion, and a detachment of R.A.S.C. with food and ammunition. We were then to break out of the bridgehead on the evening of D-Day, spend the night in Tessel Bretteville Wood, some ten miles on, and the next morning to capture the high ground near Villers Bocage, which commanded a view of the country for miles around. We were to hold on there for four or five days, when it was expected that we would be relieved by the main body of the Second Army.

The plan had been formed as a result of the failure to exploit the initial success of the Anzio landing. To our inexpert eye it had seemed a slightly presumptuous scheme in England. From the map and air photographs Tessel Brettville Wood had looked just the sort of place for a Nissen-hutted camp, where the occupants might not welcome our staying the night, and the daily intelligence reports before D-Day usually brought news of more and more tanks seen in the area. Probably we were wrong, but anyway, the original plan had to be modified. Owing to the roughness of the sea several of the Rhino ferries broke away from their parent L.S.T.'s. Only half the regiment got ashore on D-Day, the rest of us remained in our L.S.T.'s about 300 yds from the shore.

The next morning I got in touch with the Commanding Officer on the wireless from our L.S.T. He gave me a new rendezvous for the rest of the regiment; then he ordered 'A' Squadron to move there as the rendezvous was well within the bridgehead, I was slightly disturbed a few minutes later to hear the Squadron Leader report that he was held up by heavy machine-gun fire. This penetrated the armour of several of the carriers, but Corporal Billingham although wounded, drove on into the middle of the enemy position, throwing grenades, until he collapsed with a wound in the head. Soon afterwards I called up the Commanding Officer again, but he cut me short, 'Get off the air, I'm shooting Boches.'

All of us got ashore that day. After an uneasy night in a regimental harbour, the next morning, D plus 2, we began a much less ambitious form of the original Villers Bocage stakes. "A" Squadron and a squadron of tanks were ordered to capture a piece of high ground about two miles outside the bridgehead perimeter. One imagined the enemy tightly penning in the bulge, so that any move forward of the F.D.L's would draw a rain of fire. In fact, the move out was completely peaceful but after about half a mile "A" Squadron was held up by isolated parties of the enemy and lots of snipers. We were being pressed by Brigade to get on; "Use your big friends and push on" kept coming over the air to me in the rear link. So the Commanding Officer went forward in his carrier to promote progress. This he was doing successfully when the ominous words came over the air from his operator: "My Sunray has been hit." He had been standing up his full six feet plus in his carrier giving orders to the tanks, when he was shot at very short range through the thigh. This was a tremendous loss to the Regiment.

Meanwhile the rest of the Armoured Brigade had had no more luck on a parallel road. The Brigadier therefore decided to concentrate on our route, and to relieve us with an armoured regiment. There was one awful moment; two sections of carriers had been sent to clear the village ahead from the rear. This meant a wide detour, but we got through on the air to recall them. To our horror we found that the message had reached only one section. As the armoured regiment entered the village shooting all their weapons right, left and centre, the other section of carriers motored strait through the fire, from the reverse direction, with the officer standing up in the leading carrier and looking distinctly surprised. No one was hurt.

For the next week or two we continued to live up to our name of reconnaissance, but every day our patrols found progress harder. In one area a squadron had to reconnoitre the same road and the same piece of ground for five days running. Each day they found the same opposition in the same places. On the sixth day that ever-recurrent rumour 'the enemy have gone' reached Brigade Headquarters, and the Brigadier ordered the Squadron Leader to send a patrol of armoured cars down the road and beat-up any enemy left. Both cars were knocked out at once by a tank, which was in its usual place. It was extraordinary how often such a rumour, usually started by a civilian, led us into trouble.

Gradually, as resistance to the bridgehead's expansion stiffened, reconnaissance gave way to holding the line. It was several weeks before the line included some of the spots our troops had reached in the first fortnight. We were introduced very kindly into the line, starting with longstop positions, in which we were able to retain our vehicles, using the armoured cars as machine-gun posts. The first time we held a proper infantry battalion position was when we took over from an American outfit at Briquessard, near Caumont.

For the rest of the campaign we used to judge all 'black spots' by reference to Briquessard. Anything described as 'worse than Briquessard' stank. It wasn't that our casualties were heavy there – they were comparatively light seeing that it was an obvious position on a forward slope and had at least its fair share of missiles. The trouble was that for the first time we had to abandon every appearance of reconnaissance. We parked all our vehicles about two miles back, re-formed our squadrons of seven troops into companies of three platoons, and occupied an almost continuous trench system, with some very large gaps in which concertina wire had to do the job of men. We were amused to find that some of our prisoners were converted German reconnaissance troops, and very disgruntled at doing infantry work. Although we didn't appreciate it at the time, our fortnight on the line at Briquessard was first-class training. But I think that if we had been there much longer our scout troops might have lost some of their dash, which they were to need again shortly. Whenever our General visited us he was most upset about our casualties. 'This isn't really your job,' he said. 'I want you for recce-ing the crossings over the Seine.'

Soon after we were back to reconnaissance again, as the great surge forward began. We went through Briquessard, and were glad to see that there were quite a number of fairly 'high' German corpses about, which we attributed to our mortars, and the quick £300 'stonks' the Essex Yeomanry used to put on for us at night. Their Liaison Officer at our Regimental Headquarters regularly worked out for us the cash value of their bombardments.

From Briquessard, 'B' Squadron, led by Lieutenant Truman's carrier troop, carried out a textbook reconnaissance into Amay-sur-Seulles, by-passing strong opposition about a mile this side, and then moving in from a flank to take a number of Boches very much by surprise. This was followed by a series of reconnaissance actions, usually on a troop scale, as the area of operations was still restricted. Lieutenant Truman carried out another classic patrol, watched by the General from the top of Mount Pincon, and some of our infantry behind a hedge near by. Truman and the Infantry Commanding Officer had discussed who should clear up the spot of trouble ahead, and Truman had said, 'Leave it to me.' The watching infantry were so impressed by his carrier left-flanking supported by Besa fire from the armoured cars that they clapped him as he came back to report.

Soon afterwards, near Le Plessis-Grimault, Lieutenant Flint won his M.C. in a brilliant patrol with his gunner, chasing Boches in and out of houses. It was here that the Second-in-Command, having arrived at the allotted area for Regimental Headquarters and brewed himself some tea, put his cup down to remark, 'This place stinks.' At that moment a fragment of shell smashed his cup, but didn't touch him. Le Plessis must have been one of the most evil-smelling places in the Bocage, apart from Falaise. Just further on Lieutenant Williams (later killed) overtook some armoured cars of a rival regiment halted short of some suspicious-looking grass turves in the middle of the road. 'We can't get on,' they said, 'Mines.' Without a word Williams threw the turves in the ditch and drove on.

So to the Seine and over, and the most exhilarating days of the campaign. Our task was to protect the left flank of XXX Corps in their armoured dash to the Somme and beyond. We were on our own on a virgin route, anything up to seventy miles ahead of Divisional Headquarters. One beautiful morning we drove forty miles before breakfast. There were several engagements, some of them quite sharp, and we collected an enormous number of prisoners. There was a pause on the Somme, then 'C' Squadron went over a small bridge, and continued to work their way forward on the left flank against fairly stiff opposition. Here Lieutenant Laing's troop of armoured cars was caught on a long, open road by a Panther, which put a round through the mudguard of his second car. They threw out their protective smoke and fired off all their weapons, none of which could damage the Panther except with a very lucky hit. This persuaded the Panther to withdraw, though it had them at its mercy; and Lieutenant Laing drove on into the village and captured forty prisoners. It was then evening, and as he had to get back to his squadron harbour he handed the prisoners over to the local French. 'Hang on to them for me,' he said in a firm Scots accent. 'I'll collect them in the morning.' When he went for them the next day he found that the French had hanged them. 'That's what you told us, wasn't it?' They said.

There followed some easy liberation with flags and kisses, and only an occasional stray enemy. Then a convoy drive to about twenty miles short of Lille; from there we were sent off again on our own route, which was so difficult that it might have been chosen for a map-reading exercise. The advance had outrun the supply of maps from England, and all we had were a few half-inch maps, which scarcely marked the side roads we were supposed to use. However, we managed to borrow a German map, with which we guided ourselves to Houplin, a village short of Lille. Here, with his mind possibly more on map reading than on the enemy, the leading troop commander advanced confidently on the bridge. When he was about a hundred yards from it an anti-tank shell broke off his aerial. The one map showed the vestige of a bridge on the right; the leading troop, made at once for this, found it passable, and were over it and infiltrating into the village in a matter of minutes. But the opposition was stronger and more determined than we had thought. 'A' Squadron were occupied here for three days, and eventually a battalion and some tanks were needed to clear the village.

Meanwhile, 'B' Squadron bypassed this trouble, ran into some more and did great execution, and then went off the air. That night a faint but cheerful voice came up on the radio to say that they had crossed into Belgium. Only later did they reveal the details of their reception. The next day the rest of the Regiment, less 'A' Squadron, caught them up as their anti-tank guns were knocking out soft vehicles at long range on their left flank, and a carrier troop was beating-up an enemy party that had come to blow a bridge on our route.

By now it was plain that there were a great number of enemy on our left flank, and as we were making for Alost at top speed, Corps Headquarters began to feel alarm that the Germans might try to cut across the Corps route behind the tanks. We were therefore ordered to stop our advance, and hold the line of the Escaut Canal from Ghent to a bridge south of Oudenarde, a stretch of thirty-five miles with more bridges than we had troops. In fact, until we were relieved to the south we were covering fifty miles with two squadrons.

'C' Squadron to the north were able to make occasional sallies over the canal to cut off isolated detachments, and one troop made an incursion into the outskirts of Ghent. As they were shooting-up a German post the Troop Commander was hailed by a local Belgium official, and led round behind the houses to interview the German Commander and tell him to surrender. The German refused, and the battle restarted.

Just north of Oudenarde a party of twenty of 'B' Squadron were holding the bridge at Eyne, with a section of carriers, two armoured cars and one anti-tank gun. In the cold half-light of the September morning they heard shooting on the far side of the canal. Then from the mist there emerged a half-track, a 75mm, self propelled gun, two more half-tracks and about a company of infantry. When they were just short of the bridge a German Officer got out of the leading half-track and tested the bridge. Sergeant Atkinson, who was in charge of our one anti-tank gun, waited until all four vehicles were closed up. Then with four shots he 'brewed-up' all four, changing to high explosive, he attacked the infantry while the rest of the detachment let loose with everything they had. At 1300 hours an officer came under a Red Cross flag to collect the wounded. Most of them were evacuated by us. About sixty dead and wounded were counted against no casualties on our side. 'B' Squadron Leader harangued the officer in fluent German, telling him to surrender what was left of his force. The officer agreed to ask his commander, but he returned after an hour to say that he'd had instructions to carry on, as his force was bigger than ours, and so battle was joined again. But they gave no more trouble.

During the time of the advance into Belgium we took about 4,000 prisoners. Their disposal was a never-ending nightmare, as there were no cages and we had no transport to get them back to Divisional Headquarters.

Our next real engagement was in the Gheel bridgehead. 'C' Squadron under the command of the Durham Light Infantry Brigade was ordered to go over the smaller of the two bridges and reconnoitre some miles beyond. As they crossed the bridge they came under heavy machine-gun and 20mm fire from close range. All the Squadron Headquarters vehicles were holed, and soon afterwards the bridge was broken. The enemy had been reinforced during the night, and the bridgehead was only 300yds or so deep here, the infantry holding it having been continuously counter-attacked. They were overjoyed to see our armoured cars, which fought their way forward like tanks throughout the day, shooting off all their ammunition. The whole squadron did a great day's work, but the casualties were heavy.

Next we were involved in the dash towards Arnhem. 'A' Squadron made early acquaintance with the Nijmegan bridge, while the rest of the Regiment was temporarily cut in two when German tanks cut the one road north. After Arnhem we had a long spell of line-holding, as the war began to settle down for the winter. We had considerable variety, sometimes watching long stretches of river or very open ground, for which our mobility and communications were ideally suited; sometimes supporting our friends the American 101st Airborne Division; but eventually in November we had a series of ordinary infantry positions in the 'Island' between Arnhem and Nijmegan. By the time that floods drove us out of our forward positions with water washing the hubs of our vehicles, we had held the line on the extreme west of the 'Island.' On the extreme north overlooked by the high ground by Arnhem, and on the extreme east. At other times we had been in reserve in the middle. We did not have many casualties on the 'Island,' but it was a miserable place, and one's heart sank every time one crossed the Nijmegan bridge going north. We started by taking over a battalion position, and finished by relieving a brigade.

In December, to our immense sorrow, the axe fell on the 50th Division. The Regiment, thus orphaned, survived for a time, thanks to our Corps Commander, who rang up the Commander-in-Chief in my presence to say that we would be worth a brigade to him. But after holding bits of the line for the 49th and 53rd Divisions we were ordered back to Iseghem to disband. We handed in all our fighting vehicles, ammunition and petrol to various dumps. All wireless sets were removed from their vehicles, and the Quartermaster had all stores in a barn for checking. And so we were all preparing to drown our sorrows in Christmas feasting.

Meanwhile, Rundstedt had begun his offensive. At 1100 hrs on 21st December the Chief of Staff at 21st Army Group Headquarters rang up and ordered us to remobilise and move. By working night and day we were on the move, fully equipped, by 0900 hrs the next day.

We joined the armoured brigades of the 11th Armoured Division in the Ardennes, first sitting along the length of the Meuse from Namur to Givet, and then gradually patrolling farther forward, until towards the end of the campaign we had a battle ground of our own with a front of 20 miles between the Americans and the rest of the British. Day after day the armoured cars set out to find and kill as many of the enemy as they could, and daily they met anti-tank guns and tanks. And when the armoured cars could not get on, the assault troops penetrated deep into the enemy territory.

Towards the end of the campaign, frost, mines and blown bridges made further advance impossible except on foot. We were asked to investigate St Hubert, which was strictly in the American boundary. Lieutenant Spreag, on his first operation as troop leader, started by carrier. When that was blown up on a mine he transferred himself to a horse (first time on horseback). With two Belgian woodsmen he rode to the outskirts of St Hubert, then straight through it. The Bosches had just left. That night the BBC reported that British Armoured cars had entered St Hubert, and the next morning the Corps Commander sent a liaison officer to congratulate us on being the first to enter St Hubert, and would we please never go there again, as the Americans were not pleased.

The next day Lieutenant Spreag, now with Lieutenant Abercrombie, walked 20 miles through shocking country beset with mines to contact the British Divisions to the north. When they reached the Airborne Brigadier he was so impressed that he at once offered them jobs. By the end of their two-day two-man operation they had walked over 50 miles.

A day later the blow fell on us again, and we returned on our last convoy along the ice-bound roads to Iseghem to start disbanding again.

During the campaign the Regiment earned one D.S.O., eight M.C.s, one D.C.M., five M.Ms three Croix de Guerre and three M.B.E.s. In addition, our Belgium Liaison Officer received the M.C. for his work with us. Two other officers were awarded M.C.s after our disbandment.

G.H.Q. LIAISON REGIMENT: (PHANTOM)

The Regiment was a streamlined organisation for gaining information of the enemy by the use of long-range patrols either operating with the forward troops or dropped behind the enemy lines. Their wireless links went straight back to Army H Q. The Regiment was affiliated to the Royal Armoured Corps in 1944. Reinforcements were drawn from the Reconnaissance Corps. By the end of hostilities some 200 men were serving with the Regiment.

Most of the information on this 'Phantom' unit is still subject to restriction of information acts under the seventy and hundred year rule. Small units operated in every theatre of war from Europe to the Far East, including the raids on St Nazaire, Dieppe, Bruneval etc, etc. Wide use was made of pigeons to relay messages directly back to the War Cabinet in London.

At the time of the expected invasion of the UK after Dunkirk, this unit was deployed along the South coast to deal exclusively with an invading enemy. It had its headquarters at Richmond Park. The unit was a highly skilled officer–heavy reconnaissance regiment, which was to move forward and report on enemy strengths and deployments. David Niven was posted to 'A' Squadron, which was attached to Fifth Corps, commanded by General Montgomery, and stationed in the danger area behind Poole harbour. Besides their primary function, they also made themselves ready to go underground. A large stock of disguises was earmarked for distribution should the invasion prove successful, and key men were trained and schooled in the roles they were to adopt. David Niven was ready to re-emerge dressed as a parson. Many other well known personalities served in this unit:- Capt. Michael Astor, Hon. J. J. Astor, Lt. Lord Banbury, Major Lord Cullen, Lt. Peregrine Winston, Capt. Maurice McMillan, Sir Hugh Fraser and Gordon Richards (the jockey.)

David Niven was originally commissioned into the Rifle Brigade before transferring to Phantom where he attained the rank of Lt Col.

THE VICTORIA CROSS

The first ever was awarded and presented to Private W Coffey of the Border Regiment: by Her Majesty Queen Victoria in 1857, for heroism in the Crimean War. Since that date, 1,362 Victoria Crosses have been awarded, and all fashioned from a pear-shaped bronze fitment on the breach of a Russian gun captured at Sebastopol. Early this year a 3lb sliver was sliced from the 25lb remaining block, which reposes in a safe. Each of the services, keep a reserve of 12 crosses, and the Army's has been exhausted by awards to Australians in Vietnam. The Cross, is a fine quality article, wrought from a low grade piece of metal, recently valued at £1.00.

SMILE FOR THE CAMERA

Food For Thought

The virtue of all achievement is victory over oneself.

Those who know this victory can never know defeat!

REMEMBER THE FEATHERED HEROES
OF TWO WORLD WARS...

Pigeons have unfortunately been referred to as pests and disease carriers, but do we realise that we owe a great deal to these birds. Are we aware of the valuable work done by pigeons during two world wars?

A fine statue was erected in Brussels to commemorate some 20,000 Allied Army pigeons lost in the First World War; another was unveiled at Lille in 1936; a granite block more than fifteen feet high with two soldier figures and birds was presented to Berlin by the War Pigeons Association in 1932; a marble plaque was unveiled at Verdun in 1929 to commemorate the pigeon 787-15 who carried the last message from the besieged fort of Vaux in 1916.

The Scottish National War Memorial Chapel in Edinburgh has pigeons carved in stone, and in 1946 an inscribed rustic stone bird bath was dedicated in the garden of All Hallows Church, London, as a memorial to pigeons lost in the Second World War.

Official records show that hundreds of thousands of pigeons were used during World War Two; 200,000 young birds were given to the services by British racing pigeon breeders alone! Over 16,000 pigeons were dropped by parachute in single bird containers on enemy-occupied territory in Europe for use by agents. Of these only 1,842 returned to the UK.

Some of the remarkable achievements of these birds are on record at The Imperial War Museum - a two year old Grizzle Cock, Gustav was the first pigeon to arrive with information concerning the Normandy landings during wireless silence on D-Day; he was awarded the Dickin medal.

Among the other pigeons who received similar awards were William of Orange, on service with airborne troops at Arnhem – flew 260 miles in four hours twenty five minutes, of which 135 miles were over the sea. G I Joe carried a message over 20 miles in twenty minutes thus preventing the bombing by Allied Aircraft of advanced elements of the 56th (London) Division – at Colvi Vecchia. This bird was presented with the Dickin medal (number 40) by Major General Keightley at the Tower of London on 4th November 1946. White vision was instrumental in saving the ten lives of the crew of a Catalina Flying-Boat which came down in the sea on the 11th October 1943. Many other pigeons, including Winke, Billy, George and Navy Blue saved lives under similar circumstances.

So let the good that our feathered friends have done , live on......

POET'S CORNER

NAMING OF PARTS - Henry Reed

Today we have naming of parts. Yesterday,
We had daily cleaning. And tomorrow morning,
We shall have what to do after firing. But today,
Today we have naming of parts. Japonica
Glistens like coral in all of the neighbouring gardens,
And today we have naming of parts.

This is the lower sling swivel. And this
Is the upper sling swivel, whose use you will see,
When you are given your slings. And this is the piling swivel,
Which in your case you have not got. The branches
Hold in the gardens their silent, eloquent gestures,
Which in our case we have not got.

This is the safety-catch, which is always released
With an easy flick of the thumb. And please do not let me
See anyone using his finger. You can do it quite easy
If you have any strength in your thumb. The blossoms
Are fragile and motionless, never letting anyone see
Any of them using their finger.

And this you can see is the bolt. The purpose of this
Is to open the breach, as you see. We can slide it
Rapidly backwards and forwards: we call this
Easing the spring. And rapidly backwards and forwards
The early bees are assaulting and fumbling the flowers:
They call it easing the Spring.

They call it easing the spring: it is perfectly easy
If you have any strength in your thumb: like the bolt,
And the breach, and the cocking-piece, and the point of balance,
Which in our case we have not got; and the almond-blossom
Silent in all of the gardens and the bees going backwards and forward,
For today we have naming of parts.

UNARMED COMBAT - Henry Reed

In due course of course you will all be issued with your proper issue;
But until tomorrow, you can hardly be said to need it; and until that time,
We shall have unarmed combat. I shall teach you the various holds and rolls
And throws and break-falls which you may sometimes meet.

And the various holds and rolls and throws and break-falls do not depend on
Any sort of weapon, but only on what I might coin a phrase and call
The ever-important question of human balance, and the ever-important need
To be in a strong position at the start.

There are many kinds of weakness about the body, where you would least expect,
Like the ball of the foot. But the various holds and rolls and throws and
Break-falls will always come in useful. And never be frightened to tackle
From behind: it may not be clean to do so, but this is global war.

So give them all you have, and always give them as good as you get;
It will always get you somewhere. (You may not know it, but you can tie a
Jerry up without rope; it is one of the things I shall teach you.)
Nothing will matter if only you are ready for him. The readiness is all.

'The readiness is all'. How can I help but feel I have been here before?
But somehow then, I was the tied up one. How to get out was always then
My problem. And even if I had a piece of rope I was always the sort of person
Who threw the rope aside.

And in my time I had given them all I had, which was never as good as I got,
And it got me nowhere. And the various holds and rolls and throws and
Break-falls somehow or other I always seemed to put in the wrong place.
And as for war, my wars were global from the start.

Perhaps I was never in a strong position, or the ball of my foot got hurt,
Or I had some weakness where I had least expected. But I think I see your point.
While awaiting a proper issue, we must learn the lesson of the ever – important
Question of human balance. It is courage that counts.

Things may be the same again; and we must fight not in the hope of winning
But rather of keeping something alive: so that when we meet our end, it may
Be said that we tackled wherever we could, that battle – fit we lived, and
Though defeated, not without glory fought…….

JUDGING DISTANCES - Henry Reed

Not only how far away, but the way that you sat it is very important.
Perhaps you may never get the knack of judging a distance,
But at least you know how to report on a landscape: the central sector,
The right of arc and that, which we had last Tuesday, and at least you know.
That maps are of time, not place, so far as the army happens to be concerned
– the reason being, is one that need not delay us.
Again, you know there are three kinds of tree, three only, the fir and the poplar,
and those which have bushy tops to; and lastly that things only seem to be things.
A barn is not called a barn, to put it more plainly, or a field in the distance,
where sheep may be safely grazing. You must never be over-sure. You must say,
when reporting: at five o'clock in the central sector is a dozen of what appear to be animals;
whatever you do, DON'T call the bleeders sheep!
I am sure that's quite clear; and suppose, for the sake of example,
the one at the end, asleep, endeavours to tell us what he sees over there in the west,
and how far away, after first having come to ATTENTION.
There to the west, on the fields of summer the sun and the shadows
bestow vestments of purple and gold.
The still white dwellings are like a mirage in the heat,
and under the swaying elms a man and a woman lie gently together.
Which is, perhaps, only to say that there is a row of houses to the left of arc,
and that under some poplars a pair of what appear to be humans appear to be loving.
Well that, for an answer, is what we might rightly call moderately satisfactory only,
the reason being, is that two things have been omitted, and those are important.
The human beings, now: in what direction are they, and how far away, would you say?
And do not forget there may be dead ground in between.............
There may be dead ground in between; and I may not have got the knack of judging a distance;
I will only venture a guess that perhaps between me and the apparent lovers,
(who, incidentally, appear by now to have finished,) at seven o'clock from the houses,
is roughly a distance of about a year and a half.

By Henry Reed (1914-1986)

Lessons of the War (To Alan Michell)

Vixi duellis nuper idoneus
Et militavi non sine gloria

ODE TO A 'BREN'

Bren, Bren, I know not when my chance will come to use thee:
But fear not, Bren, for until then, I'll let no man abuse thee.
Thy barrel shall be daily cleaned with flannelette and rod;
Not dust nor rust shall thee encrust; I swear by Mars, the God of War,
For whom you were created. Thy piston shall be graphite greased
And Breechblock lubricated. No carbon shall besmirch thee
And retard thy leaden darts, for hour by hour I'll scrape and scour
Thy gas-affected parts.
So now dear Bren, farewell again. Return to oily rest.
I'll fold thy bipod up and place thee back within thy chest.

(From 'Tally Ho', field newspaper of the R.N.F. Regt.)

SMILE FOR THE CAMERA

If the burglar takes your cash / jewellry and leaves a valuable painting take heart –
- fair exchange is no robbery.

INVASION OF EUROPE

D. DAY - Tuesday 6th of June 1944. Code Names -

OVERLORD   –   Name of Invasion

MULBERRY   –   Name of pre-fabricated harbour

NEPTUNE   –   Name for Naval operation in Invasion

PLUTO   –   Name of pipe line under the ocean for the supply of fuel

UTAH   –   American landing beach

OMAHA   –   American landing beach

GOLD   –   British landing beach

JUNO   –   Canadian landing beach

SWORD   –   British landing beach

'H' HOUR   –   Time of beach landings

Governed by time of tides i.e. on UTAH & OMAHA 'H' Hour was 06.30am.
on GOLD / JUNO / SWORD time varied between 07.00 & 07.30am.

D.Day itself commenced at 15 minutes past midnight June 5th, when nearly 18,000 Paratroops were dropped on the flanks of the invasion beaches.

OPERATION GAMBIT

Midget submarines X23 & X20 surfaced at 'H' hour minus 20 minutes opposite OUISTREHAM near the mouth of the river ORNE (X23) and opposite the village of LE HAMEL twenty miles down coast (X20) to act as navigation markers on the surface to clearly define the extreme limits of the assault zone. These subs. measured 57ft long with a normal crew of three men now carried two extra crew in a cabin measuring 5ft 8in high, x 5ft wide, x 8ft long.

THE NORMANDY LANDINGS

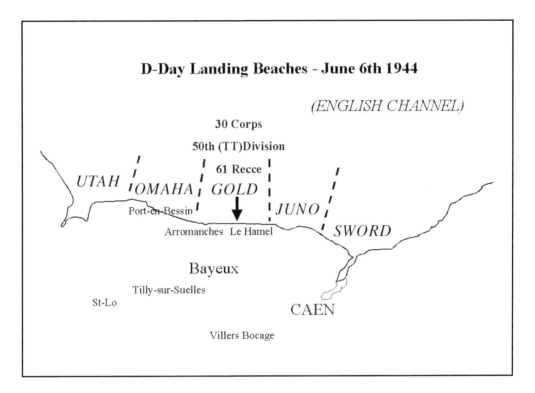

61st Reconnaissance Regiment came ashore near Le Hamel on 'Gold Beach' with 50th (TT) Northumbrian Division at around 07.00 – 07.30hrs. D.Day 6th June 1944.

Nearly half the contact patrols with the assaulting infantry were killed or wounded on D-Day, either on the beaches or before reaching them.

EMBARKATION FROM SOUTHAMPTON, JUNE 1ST 1944

In preparation for the landings on D.Day (originally planned for 5th June) it was my duty to supervise the loading of our vehicles onto the Landing Craft. This consisted of standing in front of each vehicle as it reached the loading ramp and directing the driver up the ramp in reverse gear by a series of hand signals and ensuring that each one was parked as closely as possible to each other inside the ship's hull. The order of loading was pre-arranged so the first in would be last to come out. Each vehicle had been waterproofed with rubberized canvas and 'Bostik' compound solution to prevent seawater from stalling the engine as it drove down the ramp into the sea at distances up to 3,000 yards from the shore. Exhausts and engine breather tubes had been fitted, rising several feet above the height of the vehicles to keep the engine running under these conditions.

With all other vehicles loaded into four Landing Craft it now came to the turn of my own driver to load on board but his engine failed to start. An Ordnance Officer was called and my Light Recce Car was towed away to enable others to be loaded. As our ship moved away from the dock without us we watched in anger and frustration as a Fitter worked away on our car to rectify the fault. Some time later with repairs completed we were directed to another loading ramp and squeezed on to another Landing Craft waiting to embark and join the other ships of our flotilla anchored off the Isle of White. As the last vehicle to be taken on board we were destined to be the first one to go ashore, which was not encouraging at that stage, as we were separated from the rest of our own unit, and had been loaded on to a ship containing a motley assortment of tanks fitted with 'flails' to beat the beach surface and detonate mines. None of the other troops were known to us and we were without orders, maps, or radio frequencies as all details and briefings were to remain secret until after the convoys sailed.

We remained tossing at anchor off the Isle of White until the evening of the 5th June when we set off for the Normandy coast. At that time of course we didn't even know that our destination was to be Normandy in fact. We were the first off our Landing Craft and silent prayers were uttered that our engine would not let us down again as we slid into some five feet of water and ploughed our way slowly towards the distant beach. After what seemed to be a very long time, we reached dry sand and drove under small arms fire towards the sand hills, where we were directed to head along the beach for a considerable distance until we arrived at a point where white tapes had been laid to mark an exit cleared of mines. This led us on to a small track behind the dunes and we followed this track for about half a mile when we spotted another Recce car behind a hedge in a small field. It proved to be that of Major John Cave of C Squadron and we joined him with some relief.

(Roy Howard. 'A' Sqdn.)

D-DAY (GOLD BEACH), JUNE 6TH 1944

On landing, most men found the beach obstacles the toughest part of the assault. Once through the defences, troops found the enemy opposition fierce in some sectors and almost non-existent in others. On the western half of 'GOLD' (Item sector) our patrols with the First Hampshire Regiment were almost decimated as they struggled through the water, at places up to six feet deep. They were caught by heavy mortar bursts and machine gun crossfire pouring out from the village of Le Hamel, held by the German 352nd Division. Men went down one after another. A private, George Stunell, of the Hampshire's, came across a Bren-gun Carrier standing in three feet of water, it's engine still running. Stunell climbed aboard and with machine-gun bullets whipping all around, drove it up on to the beach, when a bullet slammed into him with terrific impact. Minutes later he discovered that he was bleeding from wounds in his back and ribs. The bullet had passed cleanly through his body. It was to take almost eight hours to knock out the Le Hamel defences, and at the end of D-Day, the Hampshire's casualties totalled over 200.

To the left of the Hampshire's, (Jig Sector) patrols with the First Dorset Regiment were off the beaches in forty minutes. Next to them the Green Howards, (King Sector) landed with much dash and determination that they moved inland and took their first objectives in less than an hour. C.S.M. Stanley Hollis attacked an enemy pill-box with grenades and sten gun, permitting a rapid advance. For this and other actions of heroism on this day; he was awarded the Victoria Cross.

To the right of Le Hamel, the 47 Marine Commando, with 61st Recce units assisting, moved quickly off the beach, having lost four of their boats and having eleven damaged out of a total of sixteen, and with much of their equipment lost. They set out on a seven mile slog to take Port-en-Bassin. They expected to meet the first Yank there, but this was not to be. The Yanks were still pinned down on Omaha Beach.

From 'Gold', troops headed for the Cathedral town of Bayeux, some seven miles inland, which was reached before dark but not occupied until the next morning. Reconnaissance patrols then assembled together and, reinforced with several tanks of the 8th Armoured Brigade, formed a mobile column to break out of the bridgehead through enemy forces and drive on towards Villers-Bocage next morning.

So ended D-Day on 'Gold' beach.

(Roy Howard. 'A' Sqdn.)

SMILE FOR THE CAMERA

The Commandant of a POW Camp in Germany during the war knew that an escape tunnel was being constructed but had no idea where. He called the British leaders together and told them- 'You think I know damn nothing about the tunnel you are making. But you are mistaken. I know damn all !'

D-DAY +2: THE BULLET WHICH SAVED MY LIFE

In the account written by Colonel Brownrigg there is one slight error in his reference to the wounding of Colonel Sir William Mount.

The actual details are as recorded here –

The tanks of 8th Armoured Brigade were held up in front of a small village on our advance from the Bridgehead towards Tilly-sur-Seulles. Col. Mount came forward in his Bren-gun Carrier to assess the situation. He then drove up to my Light Recce Car and gave me orders to drive forward and go through the village at speed and await the arrival of the rest of the armoured column about a mile beyond the village in a small wood. His order was – "Show the tanks how it should be done". Normally I would have had the support of my Troop Commander in his heavy Recce Car (Lt. T.R. Compton-Bishop) but his 37mm gun had jammed and his turret was out of action, so it would have been a single vehicle operation armed with only one Bren-gun. I had to dismount and was standing examining the map with Col. Mount when he collapsed in his carrier struck in the hip by a sniper's bullet. I removed my field dressing and passed it to the Colonel who then ordered me to find Major Brownrigg (as he then was) and tell him to take over command. I instructed Col. Mount's driver to get him back to our advance dressing station as quickly as possible and then set off on foot to pass information to Major Brownrigg whom I found behind a hedge with Major Rayer (O/C A Squadron) studying the problem through binoculars. I informed them what had happened and orders were given for us to withdraw while they evaluated the situation. It was at a later stage that Major Brownrigg received the message from Col. Mount's radio operator that his 'Sunray' had been hit, the message coming through from him at the Field Dressing Station in our rear. In my mind I have no doubt that the sniper's bullet which caused a change in plan most certainly saved the lives of my crew and myself.

On the other hand – it may also have deprived me of a medal for leading the victorious charge. No-one will ever know which !

(Roy Howard 'A' Sqdn.)

MR. TREVOR LAWRENCE 7 TRP. A SQDN.

(Newsletter Old Comrades Association)

Trevor has written a long account which he says is a major point that 7 Troop A Sqdn were the only Sec. that Sir William Mount had from D-Day to when he got wounded, when we were out beyond the Bridgehead by about a couple of miles. Our Sec. consisting of 3 Carriers, myself as Sec. Sgt. Cpl Hampton in charge of another Carrier and L/Cpl Billingham.

We had to cross a minefield to get out – this we did taking a big risk, we carefully followed in the retreating German tracks, which was successful. We then travelled a couple of miles further on when we were joined by a Sqdn of Sherman tanks, I believe from 8 Brigade. We then entered a cornfield, and as we were going through it, one of the tanks hit a mine. We carried on to the far left hand corner of the field; at this point there was a wood, we then proceeded on a rough track, where we were very unfortunate to shed a track from our Carrier from the bogey. We had to split the track and lay it out straight in front to manoeuvre the Carrier onto the track, which we accomplished.

At this point I noticed a camouflaged look-out close by. We then proceeded to the edge of the wood; we were behind an earth bank, when we could see Germans running around. This message was passed back to the tanks, they lined up abreast and charged in line out of the wood firing their guns. Unfortunately the Germans opened up their anti-tank guns and destroyed nearly every tank, with turrets blown off, and tanks exploding. One tank in front of us was hit, and I could see only one wounded survivor who crawled over the side nearest to us. I took my rifle and told my section to cover me, as I went down a small ravine, which was full of blackthorn and briars. I reached opposite the tank and then had to cross open ground in full view of the Germans. I kept as close as I could to the ground.

Eventually, I got to the injured man to find that he had a leg nearly severed with the bone showing. I dressed it with my Field Dressing and then successfully carried him back to our position, the same way I entered. By then there was a stretcher, which we placed him on and gave him a dose of morphine. He was then transferred to First Aid Post. I should like to know if that poor soldier survived.

CASUALTIES SUSTAINED OVER
24 HOUR PERIOD OF D-DAY ASSAULT

Estimated at between 10,000 and 12,000

U.S. FORCES – 6,603 of which 1,465 killed, 3,184 wounded, 1,928 missing, 26 captured
Included in these figures U.S. 82nd and 101st Airborne losses estimated at 2,499

CANADIAN FORCES – 946 of which 335 killed

BRITISH FORCES – No figures ever issued, but it is estimated that casualties were at least-
2,500 to 3,000 of which 6th Airborne suffered losses of 650

GERMANS – Estimates range between 4,000 and 9,000

N.B. By the end of June, Rommel reported his casualties for the month as –

28 Generals, 354 Commanders and approx. 250,000 men

Allied Casualties by 30th June reached 62,000 dead and wounded.

BY 21ST JUNE 1944 CASUALTIES 50 (TT) DIVISION

Since D-Day the 50th Division had suffered 312 Officers and 3,662 other rank casualties, the
highest of any Division in Normandy.
Including 2 Brigadiers and 12 Commanding Officers.

Officers 65.9% wounded. Other Ranks 50%
Officers 16.5% killed. Other Ranks 8.7%

61st RECONNAISSANCE REGIMENT CASUALTIES

D-Day losses amounted to 50% in first 24 hours.
Total losses incurred up to January 1945 amounted to almost 76% out of their original
numbers either killed, wounded or missing.

N.B. Figures published in "The Sharp End of War" by John Ellis and "Decision in
Normandy" by Carle D'Este.

THE REUNION (D-DAY +5)

We had been in action as a special armoured column, during the course of which, our Commanding Officer, Lt. Col. Sir William Mount, had been severely wounded, and the 37mm gun on my own Troop Commander's car had seized up in the recoil mechanism. I was ordered to change vehicles with him and to return to Bayeux to the Ordnance Base for repairs. The return to Bayeux and the repairs took up the entire day, and while work was being carried out, I made enquiries via the Military Police, as to the location of a certain Royal Engineer Unit in which my brother was serving. The location was only some three miles outside of the town, and so soon as our vehicle was ready, I directed my driver to its position. On arrival I reported to the Unit's Duty Officer and requested permission to harbour with them overnight. I explained that I was hoping to find my brother and he told me where he was to be found. The look on his face on seeing me was one of true surprise. We had met only once throughout the war, when we had both returned from Dunkirk, since when he had travelled throughout the Middle East with the 8th Army. Within half an hour we had a mountain of chips frying over a petrol fire, and from my 'borrowed' vehicle I produced a four and a half gallon jerrican of Calvados Brandy recently 'liberated' from a Normandy brewery. A good time was had by all, and when we left shortly after dawn to re-locate our own unit, we were in convivial spirits, in spite of our thick heads. I reported that the Troop Commander's jerrican had been holed by a sniper's bullet during our travels. My brother and I were not to meet again for another two years when we had both been demobilised.

(Roy Howard 'A' Sqdn.)

Brothers Noel and Roy Howard 1939.

The Truth:- I have had many troubles, most of which have never happened!

VILLERS – BOCAGE, NORMANDY (JUNE 12TH – 14TH)

The German Tank Hero – Obsturmfuhrer (Captain) Michel Wittman

The Heavy S.S. Tank Battalion 501 was commanded by Obsturmfuhrer Michel Wittman, a tank 'ace' from the Russian front with 119 victories to his credit. The only tank available to him to block the breakthrough of an entire British Armoured Division was his own Tiger. Wittman fired one shot from his high-velocity 88mm gun and the leading British half-track stopped in a blazing ruin blocking off the road of the British advance, then the Tiger rolled ponderously forward and turned down the road towards Villers Bocage. Half-track after half-track went up in flames. Then it encountered a Cromwell tank commanded by Major Carr. The Cromwell fired point blank and for all the good it was it might have been a pea-shooter. The 88mm fired again and the Cromwell was instantly wrapped in flames. The Tiger continued down the road belching forth shot after shot. Three more Cromwells were destroyed, and in a brief five minutes Wittman accounted for 25 British tanks, 14 half-tracks and 14 bren-gun carriers! The spearhead of the British 7th Armoured Division (The Desert Rats) had been annihilated.

Now supported by other Tigers from his unit, Wittman continued into Villers Bocage. British infantry armed with Piat anti-tank weapons managed to blow off one of the tracks of Wittman's Tiger, and Wittman was forced to bale out. By nightfall the British were forced to withdraw, and Villers Bocage was not in British hands until June 30th.

(Photo – Imperial War Museum)

Wittman was killed later in the 'Falaise Pocket' on August 8th. He perished at Cintheaux after he had attacked a group of Sherman tanks head on and smashed two of them. The remaining five Shermans opened fire on him at point blank range and he and his entire crew were killed.

Prior to his death, Wittman was responsible for the destruction of 138 Allied tanks and self-propelled guns, and the disablement of 132 anti-tank guns!

(See the 'Killing Ground' – London Publication 1978)

After the failure of 7th Armoured Division to take the town, Montgomery sacked their Commanding General – Major General Erskine. He also sacked Brigadier Robert Hind, commanding the 22nd Armoured Brigade, and the Corps Commander – Lieutenant General Bucknall, all on the grounds that they had lacked the necessary 'get up and go' spirit which Monty considered may have altered the situation. All in all, Michael Wittman had had a very satisfactory day!

The 50th (TT) Division had been having an equally costly day trying without success to break through the forces of the German Panzer Lehr Division. They were held by the enemy at Tilly-Sur-Seulles and Hottot, just five or six miles from Villers Bocage which they had been ordered to reach to give infantry support to the 7th Armoured Division. The 50th (TT) Division also came in for much of Monty's anger.

Wittman's Tiger Tank in the devastation of Villers Bocage.
(Photo – Imperial War Museum)

Wittman – Addendum 1990

When Wittman was killed at Gaumesnil, south of Caen, on the 8th of August his usual gunner was not among the crew, he was absent on sick leave, and his place had been taken by a temporary replacement. The original gunner is believed to be still living.

(Roy Howard 'A' Sqdn.)

Obersturmfuhrer (Captain) Michael Wittman, the Leibstandarte tank ace, sits on the mantlet of his tiger tank's 8.8 cm: KwK 36 main gun. The tank has been coated with Zimmerit paste, a device to prevent the placing of magnetic mines on the tank sides and hull. (Photo – Imperial War Museum)

In June 1990, I was able to visit the German War Cemetery at La Cambe and leave a tribute on the grave site of this German War Hero and his Crew.

THE TRUTH

Caen, Normandy (25th June to 16th August 1944)

By halfway through the morning of D-Day, the British and the Canadians were paying the penalty for their bad weather landing. The air bombardment only partly effective; heavy casualties among the parachutists; far fewer DD Tanks reaching the beaches than expected; congestion on the beaches and at the exits; delay in passing through the fresh assault formations which were to drive deep inland. Even the capture of Caen, ten miles inland had never had better than an outside chance, and General Crocker, commanding 1st Corp, had instructed Major General Rennie, of 3rd British Infantry Division, that Caen must be captured before last light on June 6th. However, the surprise effect of a bad weather landing was immense. The overall result was that instead of Caen being taken by the end of D-Day, it was not finally taken until the 16th of August, by which time the city was almost totally destroyed. On D-Day to the west of Caen, tanks were advancing towards Cairon. They had been reduced to half strength by the beach assault, and B Squadron now numbered only nine tanks. They received a call for help from the infantry attacking Pierrepont, and swerving off the road to the attack, they moved ten yards and lost five tanks. Their end was instantaneous and dreadful, for they had stacked the floors of the tanks high with reserve ammunition, fearful that the chaos on the beaches would prevent supplies getting through. The Sherman tanks burned quickly when hit, almost instantaneously. The Germans called them 'Tommy Cookers' and the British called them 'Ronsons'- because of the trade advertisements – 'Light first time'! Of the original 18 tanks, which had landed, there were now only four tanks left. In the original plan to take the city, it had been anticipated that a large number of tanks should have rushed Caen at once, the infantry riding on the backs of the tanks, but due to the chaos on the beaches by 12.30 hours, the Shropshire Light Infantry started to walk there, minus their heavy weapons and vehicles, and without the tanks. The lightening punch at Caen had been reduced to a few hundred plodding riflemen. Across the channel in England, presses were rolling out the 'news' to announce the fall of Caen, and the complete success of D-Day with street fighting going on in the town. So it was reported in the 'Daily Express', and the 'Daily Mail' had a similar story. Where the news came from is anybody's guess.

Montgomery's seaborne HQ had no idea what was happening, with the communication centre hopelessly jammed with a backlog of undecoded messages, and in fact, there was to be no street fighting in Caen for another four weeks.

Operation Epsom (25th June - 2nd July)

On June 25th and 26th, a sand model of the proposed plan had seemed most impressive. German defences were to be hammered mercilessly by 250 bombers and a 'Monty' artillery barrage until they cracked, then the 15th Scottish Infantry Division were to pour through the gap, their flanks covered by the 49th Division. The crowning blow was to be made by 11th Armoured Division who were to race for the high ground at Baron and Hill 112. Throughout the night it rained and became a downpour, and men were saturated and without sleep prior to the attack.

At dawn, 700 guns opened fire as the 15th Scottish set off forward in the sodden terrain, but there were many hours spent waiting at the roadsides under the rippling noise of German machine guns as a threat on the right flank developed from Rauray, where 60 tanks were reported. Tanks of the 49th Division failed to appear, so did the RAF Bombers so faithfully promised, but the advance continued slowly. Cheux was cleared and St Mauvieu taken by late afternoon. The orchard area of Le Heut du Box was reached, and then trouble struck. Machine guns opened up on the leading companies and the Scottish went to ground under heavy fire. As the attack had lost direction and gone astray, the CO decided to re-group in Cheux which rapidly became a bottleneck, jammed with rubble and wrecked vehicles, and two divisions and two brigades trying to pass through one narrow street. 31 Tank Brigade with Churchill tanks went forward with the infantry, and as soon as they reached the Caen road between St Mauvieu and Cheux, 11th Armoured Division was to advance with its 29th Brigade leading – 23rd Hussars and the 2nd Fife and Forfar Yeomanry, followed by the 3rd Royal Tank Regiment as reserve. C Squadron of the 23rd Hussars by-passed Cheux to the East, although the remainder went through the village and continued through difficult country supporting the advance of the 2nd Gordons, and two companies actually got into Colleville. The rest of the Battalion were miles away, motionless in the traffic jam. On the morning of 26th, not even Fontenay was completely clear, and only half of Tessel Wood* (see 61 Recce History) had been taken. Caen had yet to be taken!

(First reached by us 61 Recce on D + 1)

Operation Charnwood (4th July – 10th July)

You will not find in any British history, official or otherwise, or in any British General's memoirs, and most certainly not in Field Marshal Montgomery's, any mention of what actually happened in Caen on the late evening of 7th July 1944. They tried a great experiment in the technique of war, and found that they had committed mass murder for nothing.

No British lives were saved. It was one of the 'minor' mistakes of war, and the corpses of men, women and children in Caen were to be numbered in thousands. The British were in fact murdering their former friends, the French! Having so failed to take the city, it was decided to make a head-on attack from the North. Three Divisions numbering 115,000 men were to assault on the morning of the 8th July, supported by a terrific artillery barrage backed up by off-shore shelling by the battleships and cruisers of the Royal Navy. General Dempsey (2nd British Army Commander) decided to try on a grand scale what had already been tried out in miniature. The intervention of the strategic airforce on the battlefield.

To take Caen it was planned to drop 2,560 tonnes of bombs on the city. Montgomery wrote afterwards that 'owing to the weather forecast' bombing was timed for between 21.50 and 22.30 hours; on the 7th July, with a gap of some six hours before the ground operations began next day at 04.20 hours. The official historian, writing still later, examined the RAF records, and the actual weather forecast for both days, and found that – 'this was not so' – Air Marshall Sir Arthur Harris demanded a safety margin between the British forward positions and the bombers aiming point of 6,000 yards.

This was accepted, and the target area, was to be a rectangular box which took in the Northern outskirts of Caen, but left entirely alone the main German defence positions, as these were far too close for comfort to the British frontline.

The theory, they were to be neutralised or eliminated by artillery fire. So was the scene set for tragedy. No 635 Pathfinder Squadron were airborne at 8.20 pm. Caen was to be done in style. The Bomber crews were quite detached from their target and there was a tendency to bomb at the earliest possible moment, then nose down and go like hell for home. With everyone doing that, naturally, the aiming point of the entire bomber stream tended to drift back after the master bomber marked the target. As the main stream bombed, the markers were soon obscured by dust and smoke. Squadron Leader (Pathfinder) Bennett was demanding but first class, and didn't agree with 'Butch' Harris, who was indiscriminate and almost regardless of whether results were possible or not. At their briefing it was stressed to the bombers – 'for God's sake don't let them drop back at all!' Flight Lieutenant Linaire got odd snapshots of what was going on in between his stints at his bomb-sight as he marked the target through intense flak as the daylight faded. From the ground the scene was awe-inspiring and terrible to watch as dust obscured the sun. A gunner officer serving with the 56th Staffordshire Infantry Division, and Lieutenant John F Brown of the 6th North Staffordshire Regiment reported on how heartened they were by the sight of 500 heavy bombers streaming in, in a long unswerving line straight over the city. Eyewitnesses inside Caen reported thousands of tonnes of bombs falling on one of the most historic cities of France. Brigadier Hill and Squadron Leader Hill (brothers) watched the raid from the beach, ten miles away. "We were not of course supposed to know, because it was not our job, but it was the general impression at that time, there were no Germans in Caen itself, all such troops being located in defensive positions outside the city boundaries. There were no services or military objectives in Caen and all the bombardment did was to choke the streets and hinder the allies in their advance." A nun wrote in her diary that there were 5,000 civilian dead in the streets, and hundreds buried in the debris, still alive. The minimum damage was done to the Germans, the vital defence zone being deliberately left intact under the plan, as it was to be smothered by artillery next day. As this artillery barrage opened fire on July 8th and the Infantry of 3 Divisions began to advance, the German Spandaus whiplashed the corn, and mortar bombs screamed down. Hidden German 75 mm and 88mm guns began firing their high velocity shells. The 2,500 tonnes of bombs dropped on Caen had had no observable effect. All it had achieved was to alert every last German soldier to the imminence of a major attack. On July 9th, the first Canadian troops entered what was left of the city.

Goodwood (18th July – 20th July)

Casualties in the action for Caen were running at approx: 3 to 1. That is 3 dead British for every dead German, and the ratio of replacements i.e. for each two men who became a casualty, there was only one replacement. Less than two weeks later there were no longer *any* replacements available, they had to be fed into units, and had themselves become casualties. The only way left to keep divisions up to strength, was to break up an existing division, already bled and shaken, and distribute the survivors piecemeal into other units. The armoured divisions had lost many tanks, but many of their crews had been able to bale out, and new vehicles, unlike infantrymen, were still in good supply. This resulted in the decision to use the armour, not the exhausted infantry for operation 'Goodwood.'

There were three armoured divisions available. The 11th, which had seen action at the Odor; the Guards, which were newly landed and inexperienced; and the 7th who were very experienced. There were 500 reserve tanks parked in Normandy, so that heavy losses could be accepted. There were plenty of tank crew reinforcements in the pipeline and more standing by in England.

The big question was where to use this force? 'Epson' had proved that the Odon/Orne front was totally unsuitable for mass movement of tanks because the roads ran the wrong way. Tanks can take to the fields, but they have to have petrol, ammunition, and workshops, and lorries are road-bound. Moving a division is like moving a small town, a difficult feat in itself, even without opposition. Also the Orne barrier meant an assault river crossing at the outset; there was also a large uncleared minefield. There was only one area where the British already had a bridgehead, east of the Orne and Caen canal. This was overlooked by the Germans holding the high ground of the Bois-de-Bavent and the Caen factory suburb of Colombelles. This area was finally decided on because it was not quite so unsatisfactory as the alternatives. So narrow was the front, that there was no room to use the three armoured divisions in line abreast and they would have to advance in line ahead, on a front only a few tanks wide. 11th, Armoured Division was to lead, commanded by Major-General Roberts, to be followed by the inexperienced Guards Division, followed by the 7th Armoured. The object was to effect a strong 'left hook' around Caen from the north-east, in an arc starting due south and ending up facing south-west and west. This left the entire flank of the narrow thrust exposed to German fire at short range for something like six miles. Both the flank, and the line of advance were held at heavily fortified villages covering each other by mutual defensive fire. On the right flank of the advance were equally heavily fortified outskirts, and factory areas of Caen: Colombelles, Mandeville, and Cormelles, before they could reach Cagny. Then, a mile ahead beyond the railway embankment, numerous villages before Bourguebus, the ultimate objective between two national highways - the N13, Paris road, and the N158, Falaise road. British and Canadian infantry were to clear the left and right flanks respectively, but would clearly not be able to pace the planned tank advance, which was to go in at speed to saturate the defences. Intelligence reported that German defences were only three or four miles deep, but intelligence reports had wrongly placed one Panzer Division, mislaid another, and did not even know of the existence of a third. It was believed that the line was held by enemy infantry, and that 21st Panzer Division was locked up in the Caen suburb of Vaucelles. More than 2000 bombers, and 720 guns with 250,000 rounds of ammunition, were to open up a secondary bombardment, and the loss of even 300 tanks would not be too high a price to pay to take the Bourguebus Ridge. This was to form the hinge upon which the American breakout could pivot when they started their breakout – already delayed until 25th of July. Villages on the left and right flanks were to receive 2,500 tons of bombs each, and the single village of Cagny, in the path of the advance, was to receive 650 tonnes of RAF bombs on it – one small village! The strong points in the centre would be swamped with small calibre bombs from the concentrated might of the U.S. Air Force. In comparison, the bombing of Caen itself on the 7th of July had been small scale. No-one was prepared for a bloody battle, and no plans had been made for such an impossible eventuality. At 05.30 hrs on July the 18th the guns began to fire, and over 1,000 RAF bombers came in wave after wave, followed by Fortress and Liberators of the U.S. Air Force. Nothing could survive such an onslaught, it was thought. How wrong they were! One of the new concepts in Normandy was the use of armoured cars for reconnaissance.

Armies were supposed to advance and retreat behind a mobile screen of these fast, wireless equipped Reconnaissance vehicles, but the Germans in Normandy proved surly and un-obliging.

The first thing an armoured car met, was either a tank, or an anti-tank gun; result no armoured car! The bombing this time attracted no flack. After July the 7th, all anti-aircraft guns had moved from the city and were now employed in an anti-tank role along the line of the 'Goodwood' advance, and dead in the path on the Bourguebus Ridge, and was not on the RAF bombing programme, and outside the range of the artillery programme. It was on the US 8th Airforce programme, but the Yanks came over in tight formation, and much higher, and proved to be scattered and ineffective in their bombing in the most vital area of the attack. Nevertheless, the plight of the Germans appeared to be appalling, and for many of the Germans it was their worst day in five years of war. Behind this barrage, the British began to advance.

(18th & 19th July)

The leading tanks moved up to the minefield at 02.30 hrs on the 18th. At about 04.30 hrs, in the grey light of dawn, the leading vehicles, consisting of Lieutenant Colonel Silvertip's 3rd Royal Tank Regiment led the whole procession through the minefield, nose to tail. The second wave consisted of R.H.Q., the Recce Troop, the Carrier Troop, the Flail tanks and half a troop of Engineer tanks, and AVREs. Between 05.47 hrs and 07.45 hrs some 8000 tonnes of bombs turned the ground ahead into a spurting dust storm, obliterating the positions believed to be held only by the 16th Luftwaffe Field Division. At 07.45 hrs, the artillery barrage began. 250,000 rounds were available, up to 750 shells were stacked beside each gun. Some of the rounds fell short, directly onto the 3rd Royal Tank Regiment, killing several commanders and wounding many crews, and they set off after the barrage in some disorder. The ground before them was pitted with bomb craters which could not be crossed, and swerving round them, they began to lose time and direction, and the tanks following, dropped further and further behind. By the time all had crossed through the minefield, and formed up beyond, they were a mile behind the leading Regiments, and not 100 yards as planned. The 3rd British Division, covering the left flank, met trouble at Touffreville, and tried to get their ambulances back. Lt Powle, controlling traffic at the bridge, let them through whenever there was a gap in the 'Up Traffic,' and was blasted for it by a Staff Brigadier. Traffic began to pile up because there was no room forward. As the 3rd Royal Tank Regiment passed between the first groups of defended villages, there was little opposition, but as they approached Manneville, they met the 'Tiger Tanks' of 503 Panzers. With orders to press on, the only thing to be done, was to fire on the move, and keep the enemies head down, leaving later troops to clear the enemy. This led to dire consequences later. On approaching Cagny where the three armoured Divisions were to radiate in three spokes, and fan out between the other two divisions, there was no infantry to take the village, having been left behind, on the Corps Commanders direct order, to clear those occupied villages now some miles behind. It soon became clear that neither bombing, nor shelling had eliminated the enemy from Cagny, and that its defenders had heavier weapons than rifles to use. Contrary to intelligence reports, the village was held by Panzer Grenadier Regiment 125, plus a part of Panzer Regiment 22, plus 'Tiger' and Heavy Tank Battalion 503, plus the special equipment of 200 Assault Battalion, - all commanded by Oberst von Luck.

In addition, the senior formation of the Waffen SS was being held in reserve on the Falaise road behind Bourgebus. Now the torrent of armour, advancing through the German lines, turned into a 'death ride.' A squadron of the British Fife and Forfar were wiped out in a matter of seconds. Twelve Sherman Tanks were knocked out, and the 23rd Hussars in their rear came to a stop behind a suddenly halted mass of vehicles.

The 3rd Royal Tank Regiment were fired upon by anti-tank guns, and from then on things became grim. One hundred and six tanks lay crippled and out of action.

The battle of Cagny began about 10 in the morning, and lasted until 4 in the afternoon, until the infantry arrived, and then the village fell almost at once. Some 200 tanks were lost, and still the enemy counter-attacked! Next day the attack went in again! The 3rd Royal Tank Regiment received eleven replacement tanks during the night, up to approx.: half its strength. It moved forward again at 04.30 hrs; and the orders were the same – to get up on the ridge. Several tanks were knocked out in the first few moments, and we were soon in the same predicament, reported Major Close, and we were completely unable to advance until about 4 o'clock in the afternoon, when field guns had been brought forward to open another barrage. The Northants Yeomanry went in first, lost direction to the right, and lost half their tanks to enemy attack from the flank. 3rd Royal Tank Regiment were then ordered to switch their attack from Hubert Folie to Bras, under cover of smoke, and managed to break through. The 3rd Royal Tank Regiment had started the day before with 52 tanks and received 11 replacements during the night, making 63 tanks in all. With Bras now in their hands, they had nine tanks left. Major Close's A Squadron had lost all Troop Officers, either killed or wounded, and only one Troop Sergeant was left. The Fife and Forfar had fared even worse. Every Regiment which had gone up that ridge had been knocked to pieces, and 11th Armoured Division was spent. The collapse of 'Goodwood' became a bone of contention in an inter-service and inter-allied dogfight. (This was more fully chronicled by Chester Wilmot at a later date.)

Total losses for the three days of 'Goodwood', for the armoured Corps only, have been put as high as 413 and does not include losses suffered by the supporting tanks of the two flank Corps; 11th Armoured Division losses for the first day only, were put at a little over a hundred tanks. The true figures were not known at the time, and never will be known.

(From – Caen, Anvil of Victory. - Roy Howard 'A' Sqdn)

THE 8TH ARMOURED BRIGADE
BREAK-OUT FROM NORMANDY BRIDGEHEAD
JUNE 7TH - 12TH 1944

(Account by Brigadier HJB Cracroft, Commander)

INTRODUCTION

During the planning of the invasion of Normandy I was warned that as soon as the initial objectives had been obtained, I should be put in command of a Mobile Column to exploit, as an independent force, with the objective of capturing the centre of communications at Villers-Bocage. I was asked to submit a plan. I had maps and air photographs to work from.

In making my plans I took into consideration the following factors:-

I wanted one or two intermediate objectives which I could hold tactically whilst I regrouped my forces if necessary.

I wanted two lines of advance, so that, if opposition or obstacles were met on one, I could switch to the other.

I wanted to avoid using main roads because I thought on these I was likely to run head on into enemy reinforcements moving forward and should get involved in battles, which would divert me from my objective.

I thought that by staying as far forward as possible I should have a shorter distance to go and a shorter line of communication to keep open.

Accordingly, I recommended my start line should be the main road Bayeux-Caen. My intermediate objectives were to be:-

Pts 103 and 102
The Tessel - Bretteville feature
High ground Northeast of Villers-Bocage.
My axis of advance was to be:-

Right road - Coulombs, Loucelles, Audrieu, Juvigny, Villers-Bocage.
Left road - Bronay, Cristot, Fontenay-Le-Pesnel, Villers-Bocage.

This plan was approved and it was decided that the Mobile Column should be formed as soon as possible after the D-Day objectives had been captured.

NARRATIVE

7th June
Due to delays in capturing some of the objectives, tanks were still fighting on D+1 and it was not until 2200 hrs that orders were issued for the exploitation forces to assemble.

We assembled during the night of 7/8th in the area Brecy-Rucqueville. The forces consisted of:-

8th Armoured Brigade TAC HQ
4/7th Dragoon Guards
Sherwood Ranger Yeomanry
24th Lancers
147 Field Regiment RA (SP) Essex Yeomanry
61st Reconnaissance Regiment
'A' Company 1st Dorsets (on cycles)
288 Anti Tank Battery (Northumberland Hussars)
'A' Company 5th Cheshires - less one platoon (MG)
RE Reconnaissance Party
Detachment 168 Light Field Ambulance.

8th June
The advance started at midday on the 8th of June.
On right axis **61 Recce Regt** supported by 4/7 DG.
On left axis 24th Lancers.
On the right we soon ran into opposition in Loucelles but after some fighting captured the village but were held up just South of it. There was strong 88mm opposition in the area where the road crossed the railway.

On the left 24 Lancers ran into very strong opposition in the area Putot En Bessin. The country here was very thick and the enemy appeared to have a number of anti tank guns we lost tanks and in spite of every effort to outflank the village it became apparent that further advance without infantry support would not be possible. Unfortunately I had no infantry for this task and accordingly I decided to abandon the attempt to break out on this axis and to concentrate all my efforts on the axis Loucelles - Pt.103, and ordered 24 Lancers to switch their attack to Loucelles. The country on this line was very thick and very built-up, and it was apparent that we should need considerable infantry support to get the tanks through it.

As my Motor Battalion 12 KRRC had been excluded from the earlier loading tables, a battalion from 131 Brigade, 1 Dorsets, were allotted to me for this role and quite magnificently did they carry it out, although they had never worked with armour before and the nearest that they came to a Motor Battalion in the matter of equipment was to have one company (A) equipped with cycles. Their CO joined my Tac HQ on the morning of the 8th and not long afterward the remainder of the Battalion moved into the assembly area at Rucqueville, where they came under my command.

I thought at this time that there was probably only a thin crust of German defence and that if I could once break through there would be no further organised resistance.

At about 1600 hrs I therefore moved 1 Dorsets into Loucelles to replace **61 Recce Regt** who were unsuitable for the dismounted fighting which was now necessary. As soon as this regrouping had taken place the advance continued and we succeeded in capturing the crossing over the railway South of Loucelles. By dark we had advanced into the northern outskirts of Audrieu.

The 4/7th DG spent an unpleasant night in Le Bas D'Audrieu with themselves at one end of the village and the Germans at the other - between them, about one hundred yards of no-man's land containing a knocked out enemy armoured car.

9th June
I ordered the 1st Dorsets, supported by 4/7th DG, to continue to advance through Audrieu and ordered the SRY to recce the open ground to the right to find out if it was possible to cross the railway West of the station. I hoped to outflank Audrieu.

I got a report that this crossing was possible and was clear of the enemy. It is of interest to note that on June 7th C Sqn of 4/7th DG had already made a recce of this crossing with a view to continuing to Pt 103 but though they had reached the railway without difficulty, two tanks of the leading troop had been knocked out by an 88mm in trying to cross it.

Meanwhile, heavy fighting was continuing in Audrieu. I again regrouped my forces and, placing 8th Durham Light Infantry, who had come under my command that morning at 0650 hrs, under command of SRY, I ordered them to move across country in a wide sweep, outflanking Audrieu, on to Pt 103 with one squadron of tanks in front and 8th DLI, I carried on with the other two squadrons. I joined SRY and we motored quickly forward into Pt 103, meeting no opposition. The enemy were so surprised at this manoeuvre that only a few shots were fired at us from Audrieu and Le Haut D'Audrieu as we advanced.

By 1300 hrs we were firmly established at Pt 103. I ordered 24th Lancers and 147 Fd Regt to move up and join me at Pt 103. While this was being done, I carried out a recce with the COs of 24th L, 8th DLI and 147 Fd Regt for an action on St Pierre.

This attack went in about 1730 hrs, supported by the SP guns of 147 Fd Regt and MG fire from 5th Cheshires. My decision to press on at once from Pt 103 to St Pierre was strengthened by a POW report that St Pierre was only lightly held.

The village in fact proved to be held more heavily than anticipated and there was constant shelling from the forward slopes across the valley, but by 1900 hrs most of the opposition in the village had been overcome.

Though 8th DLI were not able to cross the river Seulles, they covered the easternmost of the two bridges between St Pierre and Tilly Sur Seulles.

There is no doubt that we were lucky to get into St Pierre so quickly but our luck was in part due to the speed of advance which took the enemy by surprise before he had time to react effectively to the threat of our domination.

Pt 103 dominated the surrounding country to the East and South and overlooked Juvigny and Tilly Sur Seulles, which was the hub of the German opposition; Pt 103 was thus an extremely important feature. Soon after we arrived there we saw large columns of Germans moving Northwards out of Tilly towards Bayeux and Eastwards along the road Juvigny - Fontenay Le Pesnel. We attacked these columns and succeeded in stopping all further movement, but enemy opposition strengthened and a number of enemy tanks shot us up at 103 and we lost some tanks from their 88mm fire.

We had quickly realised that our tanks were out-matched by both enemy tanks and enemy anti-tank guns and that in a straight fight at anything over point-blank range, the advantage lay with the enemy every time. Our losses on Pt 103 sharply confirmed this realisation. Thus until the tanks were withdrawn from the forward slopes of the 103 feature to hull-down positions (their place being taken by a light recce screen) we suffered a number of casualties from enemy weapons firing at long range from the woods North of Tilly across the Seulles valley. The armour of the Sherman rarely resisted any armour piercing shot except at extreme ranges and when it was pierced the tank usually burst into flames almost spontaneously.

The 75mm gun, though an accurate weapon and excellent for HE, had no powers of penetration to deal with Tigers or head-on Panthers. It is true that the 17pdr was on a par with the German guns but they were strictly limited in numbers and were only carried in the thin-skinned Shermans and M10 SPs, upon which the enemy always concentrated his fire. Probably the long 75mm of the Panther was an even better armour-piercing gun than the 88mm of the Tiger, but the Panther, unlike the Tiger, was vulnerable in the flanks and the rear. The 75mm in the German Mark IV was slightly better than our own 75mm but the Mark IV was inferior to the Sherman as a fighting machine and there was a reasonable chance in an engagement of obtaining the decision. Only the German Mark III, obsolete and rarely encountered, was definitely inferior to the Sherman in every respect.

As a whole, in Normandy, the Allied armies had a vast numerical superiority in tanks and SPs over the enemy, but this superiority was difficult to exploit in the extremely close country of the Bocage, which lent itself admirably to the defensive tactics of the heavy German AFVs, by limiting the mobility of our larger and generally speedier AFVs. It was poor consolation to know that the Panther was vulnerable in flank and rear and the enemy SPs were vulnerable if located, when one was denied by the country in the powers of manoeuvre necessary to expose those thin flanks and rear in the one case and when one was only likely to locate the hidden SP by the expensive process of losing at least the first tank to come within its sights.

During the late afternoon I had reports from St Pierre of heavy enemy fire from Tilly and it soon became apparent that the Germans were holding it strongly. Similarly, armoured recce, which moved South from St Pierre, came under heavy enemy fire.

I ordered 1 Dorsets, with 4/7th DG, to move up as soon as possible to Pt 103, to consolidate its capture - if necessary outflanking and leaving behind opposition in Audrieu and the villages South of it. In fact, the capture of Audrieu had been completed by 0845 hrs.

By the evening of the 9th, St Pierre was held, the 1 Dorsets and 4/7th DG had joined me at 103, where I placed the CO 1 Dorsets (with A Company, 5 Cheshires, less one platoon under command) in charge of the lay-out of the ground defences. We had had a heavy day fighting and had succeeded in stopping all further enemy movement Northwards and Eastwards. 4/7th DG, firing at enemy Panthers moving South down the Seulles valley, had managed to knock out one at a range of upwards of 4,000 yards, with a lucky hit on the engine covers with HE. Though the day had been a success, the SRY war diary rather plaintively records, "the days are very long". During the evening I issued orders for holding the ground we had won. The 8th DLI, with one squadron 24th Lancers in support, were ordered to hold St Pierre. The 24th Lancers less one squadron were ordered to hold the West and Southern part of 103, with 1 Dorsets holding the Southeast, East and Northeast, with 4/7th DG in support. The SRY I ordered to move back to the area Brecy so that they could re-form, re-fit and get some rest. It became apparent towards the evening that the enemy had moved back into Le Haut D'Audrieu.

The night was passed rather uncomfortably with considerable enemy mortaring of the 103 position. 3Plt of 5th Cheshires had a particularly unpleasant encounter. An enemy patrol in two parties approached the Platoon's position at Pt 103 and when the first party was challenged its members threw up their hands in surrender. Rather unwisely, on seeing this, three privates went forward to bring in their prisoners when, without warning, the second enemy party opened fire, inflicting wounds from which all three men subsequently died. However, the Platoon's guns opened up on the patrol, killing three and wounding others, before the remainder surrendered - a total of two officers and twelve men.

10th June

I had hoped to be able to continue the advance southward to my next objective Tessel-Bretteville feature but it soon became apparent that enemy opposition was stronger than I expected. On looking back at it now in view of the large enemy columns of both tanks and infantry, which we had halted the day before, it is not surprising that this opposition was strong.

In the early morning I got a report that the enemy were counter-attacking St Pierre and for a short time the 8th DLI were driven out but they counter-attacked at first light and we succeeded in reorganising and by re-attacking with the 24th Lancers, St Pierre except for the southern and western portions was recaptured and the 8th DLI re-established by 1130 hrs. during this time another enemy counter attack had come in from the direction of Cristot but this was driven off by 1 Dorsets and 4/7th DG.

During the morning I also got reports of bodies of enemy infantry moving in towards 103 from the West, i.e. from the area Buceels and St Bazire. I dealt with this by ordering the SRY to move up from Brecy and by clearing the area South of the railway and up to the river NW of 103. SRY linked up with 24th Lancers in St Pierre, after having made contact with elements of 7th Armd Div who were driving South from Bayeux to Tilly but were unable to get beyond Buceels.

By the afternoon all counter attacks had been driven off, with an estimated loss to the enemy of 2 Tigers, 4 Mark IVs and 3 75mm SP guns, and most of St Pierre was again in our hands.

I realised however that the situation on Pt 103 was going to be rather uncomfortable and I was anxious to avoid if possible the heavy mortaring to which we had been subjected the night before. The only way in which it seemed possible to achieve this was to send out patrols to try and drive the enemy further away from us out of mortar range.

The 8th DLI were fully committed in St Pierre and the 1 Dorsets who had had very heavy fighting ever since landing were committed to holding the vital 103 feature. With all of my infantry committed I only had tanks available for patrols. I accordingly ordered SRY to send out squadron patrols in the East and Southeast direction and gave them the support of 147 Fd Regt. These patrols soon made contact with the enemy and succeeded in inflicting quite a lot of casualties as well as finding good targets for the artillery. I think they paid a handsome dividend.

That evening I ordered the SRY to relieve the 4/7th DG in support of 1 Dorsets and to relieve 24th Lancers on 103. I moved the 4/7th DG back to the area Brecy to rest and re-fit. I move the whole of 24th Lancers into St Pierre as the 8th DLI who had had heavy casualties needed strong support and I was anxious not to lose the village again.

After the fighting we had been through it was obviously necessary to bring up ammunition and petrol; food, of course, was also necessary. I had had assembled during the morning a column of some 60 lorries in the area of St Leger, ready to move forward whenever a favourable opportunity occurred. This column was moved forward in the early afternoon after the SRY had cleared up the area NW of 103. As it moved up under tank escort, it was subjected to some small arms fire from the Audrieu area into which the enemy had again infiltrated. There were no serious casualties however. Supplies were delivered and the column returned again under tank escort, taking back wounded amongst whom was my Brigade Major.

When the supply column arrived an American officer came with it in a jeep. He said he was a liaison officer from the American 155mm Regt and he asked if I would like any heavy artillery support. As can be imagined I was delighted to see him and gave him a number of targets which were out of range of my own 147 Fd Regt.

During the afternoon I also got an offer of support through the Commander 50th Div of fire from a battleship. I again indicated a number of targets and we were delighted to see some good shooting with 15" guns. This was directed by an air OP.

11 June

In spite of our patrols we had another uncomfortable night from enemy mortar fire. It was heavy and went on nearly all night.

The Commander 50 Div came up and visited 103 and discussed the situation and decided that in view of the strength of the enemy against us it was quite useless at the present to try and push out further South. He therefore instructed me to hold the 103 feature and St Pierre if possible.

Meanwhile 69 Bde were to hold on my left from Pt 103 Northeast to a wood between Bronay and the Bayeux-Caen road, (892731) and 1 Dorsets were to be relieved in the evening by 5th East Yorkshires.

Southeast of Pt 103 lay the high ground round Pt 102 just South of Cristot; to command these two points was to be in control of the whole area round about for several miles. In order, therefore, to try and relieve the pressure on our left and to keep the enemy from carrying out close reconnaissance of our positions, an attack was organised for the evening to capture Cristot and to push on beyond it to capture Pt 102.

In the morning in preparation for this attack, I ordered 4/7th DG to carry out a reconnaissance in force. B Sqn and the CO reached the village and saw a great many infantry about but met no organised resistance. The probability is that they disorganised an enemy counter-attack as it was forming up; but also that the enemy were thereby forewarned of the impending attack in the evening.

This attack was to be carried out jointly with 69 Bde. 69 Bde were to direct 7th Green Howards on Bronay to secure my left flank and to make contact with the 3rd Canadian Division at Putot-En-Bessin. I was to command the attack on Cristot with 6th Green Howards under command supported by 4/7th DG, 147 Fd Regt, A Sqn 24th Lancers and A Sqn SRY. SRY were patrolling South and Southeast of Pt 103 and I ordered A Sqn to work Northeast to Pt 102 to provide right flank protection for the attack and to gain observation of the Juvigny - Fontenay road.

At 1700 hrs the 6th GH passed through 1 Dorsets in the attack on a two company front with one squadron in support of the leading companies, one squadron moving with the reserve companies and one squadron ready to escort the Bn support weapons to their objective. The guns fired on known targets and one hedge ahead of the advance.

I gave the CO of 6th GH permission to use his discretion about withdrawal and in the event the tanks of 4/7th DG just managed to reach the outskirts of Cristot and the infantry one field short of the objective, but both suffered heavy losses in the process and it was obvious that Cristot could not be captured without severe casualties in men and tanks. Added to this a strong enemy attack with Tiger tanks against Pt 103 had developed South at the axis of advance and threatened it. The attack was therefore called off and both infantry and tanks retired within the Pt 103 position.

Though the attack had failed to capture its objective, my main object had been to relieve the pressure on Pt 103 and drive the enemy further away. This we had achieved and it is possible that the attempt broke up an enemy infantry attack designed to coincide with their armoured attack on Pt 103. This armoured attack I will deal with separately below. Even if we had captured Cristot, I doubt if we should have been able with the forces available to have held it, as I could not afford to risk losing the vital 103 feature. 69 Bde to the North just failed to reach Bronay but established themselves along the main road North and South through Audrieu, thus giving secure flank protection to my positions on 103.

Certain lessons were to be learnt from this attack. It occurred at a time when the Army's initial advance was losing impetus and the contact battle was merging into static warfare; the enemy was recovering from his first shock and was fighting to the death. Though not deeply entrenched he was using the thick, close, natural cover of the Bocage - hedgerows, sunken roads, ditches, orchard and woods. In this thick leafy country the advantage is with the defenders who can stay still and hold their fire until the last moment - tanks are blind.

This attack showed that in close country tanks cannot lead the infantry - they must advance side by side - and even in more open country the best support that the tanks can give is from a position slightly in rear or to the flank. In this attack in close country the tanks and infantry quickly lost contact and their mutual protection; the tanks became victims of the anti-tank guns and the infantry the victims of the spandaus which opened up as the tanks passed forward out of reach and sight of the infantry. B Sqn 4/7th DG returned with only two out of the 9 tanks with which they began and, despite 25 - 30 prisoners taken, 6th GH suffered proportionately heavy casualties. So much for the action on Cristot. I now turn to the sequel from which I think the enemy also may have learnt some similar lessons.

During the afternoon I attended a conference with HQ 7th Armd Div which had been ordered to move up on my right flank and capture Tilly exploiting forward if possible to capture Villers-Bocage. They reached the Northern outskirts of Tilly about 1700 hrs.

I was to carry out a simultaneous attack to assist them. At the conference it was decided that 8th Armd Bde should attack and capture Tessel - Bretteville feature so as to assist 7 Armd Div and protect their left flank. I returned from the conference about 1800 hrs. as I came up the track from Chouain in my scout car I heard very heavy firing from 103 and a lot of 88mm shells whistled over my head. I arrived on 103 to find a very heavy German infantry and tank attack was coming in from the direction of Fontenay-Le-Pesnel. It was the only German attack of its sort that I ever saw and was in the approved style of infantry and tanks coming in together. Our tanks were severely handicapped because the Germans were supported by a number of 88mm tanks which were standing off and shelling us with great effect from rather long ranges - the shells burst in the treetops and created a shrapnel effect on those below. The only tanks, which we had, that could penetrate them were a very few 17pdr Shermans. Most of the five of these that we had per Regt were already knocked out.

For a time the situation was extremely tense. To add to the confusion, just before the enemy attack began, a second supply column had reached the 103 area and was "milling" about, generally in the way. I ordered it to retire at once and at speed. The tanks on the forward edge had to withdraw slightly under cover of smoke. The flashes of their guns mingled with the tracer of enemy shells and in the middle of it all an ammunition truck and an SP gun were hit and caught fire. About four tigers actually reached the position and for a short while pandemonium reigned. But at last they were driven off. In all, the enemy had used some 18 tanks mostly Tigers with a sprinkling of Mark IVs.

I went up to see the CO of 1 Dorsets who were quite magnificent and were holding their ground very firmly in spite of heavy casualties which included practically the whole Orderly Room staff. After some severe fighting which lasted until 2230 hrs we managed to drive off this counter-attack and remain in position but in doing so had had heavy casualties both to our infantry and tanks. The enemy retired under cover of smoke.

Meanwhile the day had been one of shelling for the 8th DLI in St Pierre. In the late afternoon I ordered C Sqn SRY to probe South in support of 7th Armd Div with whom 8th DLI were trying to gain contact but they were held up by tank and anti-tank gun fire. Enemy tank movements had been reported constantly and they were known to be West of the village on the far side of the Seulles bridge. During the evening the 8th DLI and SRY positions were heavily shelled and were under constant spandau fire from the high ground to the South.

At 2050 hrs the St Pierre sector received its share of the enemy armoured attack and for a time was cut off from the main Bde position on the 103 feature. The CO of the 8th DLI had to abandon his jeep and make a hazardous journey back from a conference at Bde HQ on foot through the maelstrom. The attack however was not pressed and by dusk the enemy had withdrawn.

The enemy attack had delayed the relief of 1 Dorsets by the 5th East Yorks from 69 Bde and this relief was not completed until midday on the 12th. We reorganised ourselves in for the night. Altogether an eventful and unpleasant Sunday.

12th June

We again had another uncomfortable night. I think, however, that our attack had achieved some success, as the enemy mortaring was less intense and more inaccurate than previously. The night before I had issued Warning Orders for the attack on the Tessel - Bretteville feature. A further conference was held and detailed orders of the attack were issued. The attack was to start from St Pierre with the first objective the high ground overlooking La Caude Rus. The second objective the road Juvigny - Fontenay-Le-Pesnel. The attack was to be carried out by 24th Lancers and SRY with elements from 8th DLI. On our left we could hear and see part of 7th Armd Div attack which appeared to start well but soon came up against very strong opposition in the Northern outskirts of Tilly. Our attack from St Pierre went in during the morning but the leading tanks soon came under very strong fire from enemy tanks. The main difficulty was due to the fact that we were going in with both flanks in the air. To counteract this in some measure A Sqn SRY again worked towards Pt 102 and found that some Tigers and Panthers had moved up into the woods during the night. The enemy infantry lying low and firing Piats from close range knocked out some tanks belonging to 24th Lancers. We succeeded in capturing the first objective but any advance beyond that was quite impossible.

The 7th Armd Div were completely held up North of Tilly. We held the first objective until late in the afternoon hoping that 7th Armd Div would succeed in capturing Tilly and would thereby relieve some of the pressure on our front. When it became apparent that Tilly was not to be captured I withdrew 24th Lancers and SRY back into St Pierre.

Meanwhile 69 Bde with 6 and 7 GH and 5th EY made a rather optimistic attack on my left flank in the wooded area between Cristot and St Pierre and suffered very heavy casualties.

Following orders that 50 Div were to hold the line from Pt 103 - La Belle Epine and would contain the enemy on this front, under direct orders from the Commander 50 Div and much to my regret in view of the struggle that St Pierre had cost me, I ordered 24th Lancers to cover the withdrawal of 8th DLI from the village.

With 69 Bde holding Pt 103 with 5 EYs and the road to Loucelles held by 146 Bde who had relieved 69 Bde in that area, the whole scene of the operation of the mobile column was static. There ceased to be a raison d'être for its existence and it was disbanded in the evening. I ordered the 4/7th DG and SRY to move back just South of Bayeux to rest while I remained in support in the 103 area with Bde HQ, 24th Lancers and 147 Fd Regt. For the first time since we had reached Pt 103 we had a comparatively quiet night.

CONCLUSION

My original objective had been Villers-Bocage and my object interdictions to prevent the movement of enemy reinforcements into the bridgehead at a time when it was vitally important that the bridgehead should be enlarged to give space for manoeuvre and the build up of forces. In fact, by capturing the 103 feature dominating as it did the road centres of Tilly and Juvigny I was in time to place an effective check on the movements of enemy troops to the North and East, without the necessity of reaching the Villers-Bocage area. However the appreciation by 50 Div that, as the threat of the advance of 7 Armd Div round the enemy's West flank made itself felt, it was quite possible that the enemy would withdraw from the front particularly on our right proved over optimistic.

We were up against picked troops from the Panzer Lehr, 12th SS Panzer, and 21st Panzer Divisions and they fought with fanatical determination. The incident with the 5th Cheshires shows that they were also treacherous and cruel enemies; this was even more strongly endorsed when 1st Dorsets found rows of Canadians from the 3rd Canadian Div laid out behind the chateau at Pabie. These men had been fighting in an attack on Bronay and after capture had been foully murdered by the 12th SS Division. Mercifully for us the enemy had little artillery other than anti-tank SP guns in the area although the 88mm HE shells and their mortars seemed at times to be a very adequate substitute.

Though our casualties in men and tanks had been severe I have no doubt that the operation paid a sound dividend. The movement of enemy reinforcements was checked, severe casualties were inflicted on him and we ourselves learned valuable lessons about the problems of warfare in the Bocage - in particular the need for the closest infantry and tank co-operation in the attack.

(Account by Brigadier HJB Cracroft. Commander - 8th Armoured Brigade)

MEMORIES OF BRIQUESSARD

by Roy Howard 'A' Sqdn

Prior to the invasion break-out in Normandy, we had been withdrawn from a Reconnaissance role and ordered to take over a sector of the front, from the American infantry. Leaving all our vehicles under guard, some distance in the rear, we adopted an infantry role and moved up on foot to take over a position held by the Americans in the woods at Briquessard. The position consisted of a series of trenches, reminiscent of World War 1, dug into the forward slope of a wooded hill, facing across open country to the enemy position. The changeover took place during the night in order not to alert the enemy that the Yanks had been replaced. We maintained this role for about ten days during which time we experienced all the discomfort and deprivation normally only endured by the P B I (poor bloody infantry). During that ten days we suffered considerable bombardment from enemy 'Nebelwerfer' (multi barrelled mortar) and normal mortars, pre-set to explode in the form of air-bursts to shower down on our trenches. On one of the days we received an order from our HQ Intelligence Section to send off a foot patrol to cross no-man's land and obtain positive identification of the enemy unit holding the opposite ground. One Officer, one Sergeant (myself) plus Lance Corporal were detailed to carry out this operation and we set out after dark to crawl across the open ground, to our front towards a hedge, behind which lay the German lines. We covered the distance, some 300 yards, without incidence and located a gap in the hedge. Cautiously crawling through the gap we soon came across some of the enemy force lying asleep beside their weapons. It was quite impractical to try and snatch a prisoner without raising the alarm. This had been our original intention. Instead we quickly and silently disposed of one of the enemy and stripped his body of his uniform jacket which carried badges identifying his unit formation and rank and withdrew in silent haste back to our own lines. We were able to identify the enemy as that of the SS Panzer Grenadier Regiment and the jacket with the report of our patrol were sent back to our HQ. We (the patrol) were very relieved to have returned without incidence and settled down to wait for the inevitable retribution, which would follow the discovery of our action. This came within minutes of dawn breaking and lasted intermittently throughout the whole day. The following day we received another request from HQ. Their intelligence led them to understand that the SS Grenadiers were some miles away being held in reserve against the expected American break-out, and they ordered us to carry out another patrol that night to obtain further evidence in support of our earlier findings. On the basis that the first patrol, were the most experienced men for the job-we same three were again detailed for the job to be carried out the following night.

We set out once more at a much later hour this time – I can't be sure – but I think it was around 2 am. This time we left our lines from a different point with the enemy contact position almost a ¼ mile away from our first operation. We had almost reached the German positions when heavy machine guns opened up from our rear, the tracer bullets passing only inches above our heads as we crawled forwards. No-one at our HQ had bothered to tell the machine gun regiment in our rear that we were out on patrol and the guns brought the enemy to life like no-bodies business. They opened fire in return and set up very lights to see whether an attack was imminent.

The three of us were immediately visible less than 100 yds from the enemy's line and grenades showered down towards us. Lance Corporal Hampton was critically wounded in the chest, but was the only casualty. Grabbing him by an ankle each we dragged him back towards our own lines and eventually reached cover and later on safety.

Lance Corporal Hampton was evacuated without delay and although severely wounded he in fact survived - much later becoming Mayor of Evesham in Worcestershire – but that's another altogether different story. He also became a Knight of St John but again it is another story. The Lieutenant was killed much later in the Ardennes campaign, and I suffered only a perforated eardrum which was patched up by an MO and although troublesome it didn't keep me out of further action. Our CO was furious about the machine-guns opening up behind us and he took the matter up without delay with HQ Intelligence for not co-ordinating the operation which they had instigated. So much for the top brass who were never much in favour with us lesser mortals!

(Roy Howard 'A' Sqdn)

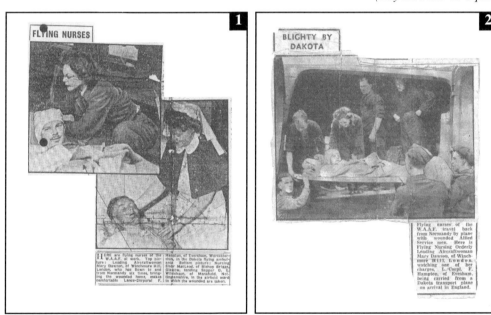

1. Here are flying nurses of the WAAF at work. Top Picture; Leading Aircraft Woman Mary Dawson, of Winchmore Hill, London, who has flown to and from Normandy six times, bringing the wounded home, makes comfortable Lance Corporal F Hampton of Evesham Worcestershire, in the Dakota Flying Ambulance. 2. Flying nurses of the WAAF travel back from Normandy by plane with wounded Allied Servicemen. Here is Flying Nurse Orderly Leading Aircraft Woman Mary Dawson, of Winchmore Hill, London, watching one of her charges, L/Corpl F Hampton, of Evesham, being carried from a Dakota transport plane on arrival in England.

Newspaper cuttings from the time showing Frank Hampton stretcher bound.

BRIQUESSARD WOOD

(Newsletter Old Comrades Association)

Thank you for your letter and glad to hear you find the Newsletter of interest. You mention – I quote "that when you were in Tilly-sur-Seulles (driven by your brother-in law) you visited the Military Cemetery and quite by chance saw "Chippy" Carpenter's grave, also those of John "Enoch" Slater and John Tootell. "Enoch" as he was known was killed at my side at Briquessard and John Tootell in the same wood a few days earlier. I remembered fishing him out of the River Bann at Coleraine, for he wasn't a good swimmer and wondered why I came so close and yet was spared. They were aged 21 like me – Tprs Slater and Tootell were '1060 boys' from the North West and I was born in South Wales."

Pete Hussey informs me Bob that Tprs. Turner and Wade are also buried at Tilly-sur-Seulles, but Sgt. Carpenter who was killed in action on 10th June '44 is buried at Bayeux Cemetery.

Mr. Bob Wilkinson C.Sqdn.

ACTION REPORT :- BRIQUESSARD WOOD

(Newsletter Old Comrades Association)

I'm Gordon Minney, HQ Signals and a later 'A' Sqn rear link with Captain Chapman. It's nice to read of old things and sometimes see names you know. My best pals were Ken Lane and Ted Evans, both Signals, but because I was hit in Holland and left suddenly, I lost contact.

I do remember one thing about Briquessard Wood. With the hot meal brought up in the evening were also rifle oil and rum, contained in old pint bottles. Ken Lane and myself were at 'A' Sqn Command Post which was built with usual tree trunks very neatly by the Yanks before we came. As each Troop came in and took their food container, oil and rum, we having put ours aside till later. Anyway, when everyone had gone, just our own two bottles were left at the bottom of the big tree from where we had issued, so I smelt one of them. It was rum and I picked up the other bottle thinking it was oil. But when I opened it, it was in fact rum as well. I hope if I confess now I will not be put on a charge – (and I wouldn't bet your haversack straps on that too much if I were you: Ed.) – but Ken and I drank the lot and next morning we didn't hear anything of the morning greeting that Jerry used to give us……

All the best, Gordon Minney.

(Thanks, Gordon; wonder how many will hang over that tale!)   *Ed. TT41*

BRIQUESSARD WOOD - JULY

Baneful Briquessard
Dank and drear,
Even at
This July year,

Patrols prowling
Cross and Cross
Lightning bursts
Catch listening posts.

Moaning Minnies'
Sobbing song
Within the ranks
Strikes out its note.

Hushed are trees as
Troops stand-to;
No nightingales
To sound curfew.

Beat of baton:
Silence stops,
While Jerry's ration
Horse clop-clops.

Frank Harding

BATTLE ACTION: - NORMANDY 1944

(Newsletter Old Comrades Association)

You will have read of the happy reunion of Sgt. Charlie Wells and Trooper Sam Benson at the Oxford Dinner after nearly 26 years. Charlie last saw Sam in Normandy, 1944, and this Dinner was their first meeting since that time. Charlie, although naturally reticent, was ultimately persuaded to recall the incident of that fateful day, and we are now pleased to relate the story:

The particular day would have been the 15th June 1944, D-Day plus 9, map ref. anyone's guess.

The action mid-afternoon, difficulties having already been met at the same point on a morning recce. Overall, quite a hectic day and one never to be forgotten by the combatants.

So the story starts then with a familiar headset signal: "Hello Able Charlie etc. Go investigate X-rds. map ref. – send infantry, roads now clear…Roger". Having positioned ARC (Armoured Recce Car) coverage, Charlie and Sam set off on foot. Up the ditch, keeping low, with pulse rate nice and even, then to a British K.O'd tank where Charlie had been fired upon in the morning scuffle and on to a hole in the hedge through which they proceeded. Now out of their ARC's cover so on their own hereon.

The objective was 100 – 150 yards away and the enemy, if still there, should have been on the right, across the road. After crawling through the grass, heartbeats now racing at full speed, they eventually reached the grass mound on the edge of the X rds and gave a look over. All was quiet, but they decided to have another look. Again raising themselves on elbows and stretching necks, lo and behold, two Germans were doing the same in unison – and a rifle's length in front of them! Had they shouted, the Germans might well have collapsed – but not a sound. And not six inches from their noses, in the grass side, was a weapon pit containing the German Spandau machine gun.

As Sam and Charlie lay there, each now knew that the X-rds were far from clear and now had to get the infantry back. As they hurriedly made their way back through the grass, the Germans opened fire with the "most frightening squirting firepower" – bullets spitting up the earth in current bun design round them as well as (or so it seemed) bullets flying between legs and arms and over shoulders. Charlie fell over three times: one mad nightmare, he recalls.

Just as they reached a spot opposite the hedge hole, Sam cried out that he was hit. Charlie dashed back to the ARC, radioed Control, and set the 37mm gun on the German position. Sam had now been sighted, and with gunner Harry Warner and driver Ray Musto manoeuvring the ARC for cover, Charlie collected Sam from the ditch where he had managed to crawl. Then Sam, cradled in Charlie's arms, was taken by carrier to an infantry first aid post where it was found that Sam had severe bullet wounds in the stomach. Although in obvious great pain, Sam, consoled by Charlie, managed to remain cheerful, but as the ambulance drove away, Charlie could only stand and stare: he just felt so lost and depressed and in that mood it was that he handed Sam's WD watch into stores, Sam's last request.

Charlie next heard of Sam about a year later in Catterick. Doc Jarvis at a later reunion confirmed Sam was OK...... and of course their meeting at Oxford 1970 is where we came in......

Thank you Charlie for the narrative and perhaps in time to come other comrades will let us share their battle experiences.   *Ed. TT41.*

Major Frank Harding reports that he came on that scene when Sam was lying on the ground after Charlie had brought Sam to safety. This would have been typical of Charlie – always sparing no effort for his men. Charlie was at the time fully capable of completely taking over as Officer in charge when no Officer available, whenever that occasion arose, also much to his credit.

SMILE FOR THE CAMERA

Dear Sir,

The saying about not being able to teach old dogs new tricks is ridiculous. For example, my uncle lives in Twickenham and whom his neighbours have always thought of as being quite unmusical, is now learning to play the cornet at 76! - What do you say to that?

Tough luck on the people at 74 and 78!

JERUSALEM

South of Bayeux in Normandy lies a very small village by the name of Jerusalem, and at a farm just outside the village there lie a number of men killed in a battle for a German strong point.

After the war, the War Graves Commission went to the location to remove the bodies for reburial in an official cemetery.

The farmer who owned the land refused to permit it saying –

"These men fought for my land, died on my land, and they shall continue to lie in my land." –

They still do!

Jerusalem War Cemetery in 1990

THE UNKNOWN SOLDIERS AND MY RADIO OP

Shortly after the break-out from the beach-head, I was sent out to try and locate the position of some enemy mobile artillery, which had been causing a problem to our infantry support. As we crossed our start line we came across two dead infantrymen and I ordered a halt while we picked up their weapons and ammunition boxes of spare magazines. They had been caught in a mortar barrage and were lying side by side in fearful solitude. One was a member of the D.L.I. (Durham Light Infantry) and the other a man of the Dorset Regiment. I was neither shocked nor horrified by the sight they made - both bodies had been torn open by bomb splinters and their intestines lay in a large pile between their legs. I wondered how it was possible for such a quantity of intestine to be coiled into so small a space as the human abdomen. The sight was not sickening or repulsive to me, but I had a deep sense of regret that these men had died with out knowing anything of the results, which their efforts had helped to achieve.

Two unknown soldiers who had made their own sacrifice toward the early stages of the liberation. We re-mounted and drove on our way into enemy territory. A few miles further and a shot rang out. Our gunner / radio operator Trooper Palmer had been killed by a sniper's bullet and he collapsed on the floor of the Recce. car. The sniper had got him directly through the head and he must have died instantly. We sought the cover of a clump of trees and there, the driver and I laid him to rest in a shallow grave, wrapped in a ground sheet, tied together with the laces taken from his own boots. We marked the spot with a branch hacked from a tree and tied his beret with the Recce. cap badge to the branch in the hope that his remains would later be recovered for proper burial. After making a note of the map reference and saying a sad farewell, I ordered the driver to resume our course and we continued our journey wondering which of us might be next.

It was a sad and miserable day and it was the first member of my crew to fall to the enemy. I can't recall whether or not we ever located the self-propelled guns but as far as we were concerned the mission had been a great tragedy.

The radio crackled intermittently and eventually the voice of our Squadron Commander penetrated my dulled brain. "Hello Fox 7 Able - report progress, Fox 7 Able."

I continued to ignore the signal for some time but eventually I pressed the transmit button and spoke - "Fox 7 Able, message received, delayed by opposition. One casualty continuing patrol, Fox 7 Able, over and out!"

N.B. 40 years later I tried to find out whether his body had been recovered. His name is inscribed on the list of missing, on the memorial at Bayeux War Cemetery but he may well be resting there marked by one of the many stones inscribed -

"An Unknown Soldier of the 1939-45 war."

I hope he's there among so many of our Recce. Band.

(Roy Howard 'A' Sqdn)

ADOLF'S LAIR: - BERLIN

(Newsletter Old Comrades Association)

(From – Captain Gordon Chapman 2nd in Command 'A' Sqdn.)

"When we moved into Berlin, I was in the leading vehicle of the British Convoy accompanied by Willie Forrest of the News Chronicle; Selkirk Panton of the Daily Express, and Bob Cooper of the Times. I arranged these three because they all spoke Russian and also knew Berlin well. At the first place where we came upon the Russians they had not finished building a river bridge, and we had to wait quite a while whilst they chopped down more trees to make the road across. Got a pretty surly reception in any case, but after a while we got past… We eventually reached Berlin and before I could get out of the Humber, a German woman rushed up, and in perfect English and tears in her eyes, said "Thank God you have come to rescue us from these barbarians." Blow me down if the next person to approach didn't say just the same thing. We talked to him for a few minutes and he told us of some of his troubles, including the price of food. If I remember rightly, meat was about £150 per kilo and others in proportion. However, we swanned around the ruins for a short while and then made our way to the Reich Chancellery, where we were met by the Russian Guard, with fingers on their triggers until we spoke to them in Russian, after which we were treated as honoured guests and given an extended escorted tour….. Needless to say, we first went down the bunker but didn't take much from it. The correspondents took signed photos of Generals that they had known personally, but I couldn't touch a thing myself. We were the first non - Russians to go down the damn thing, but a couple of French soon followed us. Missed a big opportunity then I am afraid, because the Red's hadn't even taken the Old Masters down from the walls; and you may remember that it was weeks later that somebody forced a draw and found Eva Braun's photograph album, which he later sold for a fortune. All very sordid, I thought at the time. However, the Russians bustled around when they found that I was interested in collecting (or liberating) German medals. The department had received a bomb straight through the middle (it exploded lower down) and there were thousands of medals around. The Russians had only liberated the really big cases, probably Knights Crosses with diamonds etc; so I was able to get about sixty or seventy different types, with a few doubled up. They didn't do me any good however, as about a year after I was demobbed the window cleaners stole most of them, and I now only have the replacements which they kindly left behind.

Gordon Chapman.

Most interesting to have a first-hand report – and it would also be interesting to know if these window cleaners ever missed a rung!   *Ed. TT41*

N.B. When the 61st Regt: broke up in Izagem, Captain Chapman went to No.5 Public Relations Service Unit which provided Escorts etc: to War Correspondents, Radiomen, etc.

NORMANDY REVISITED

(Newsletter Old Comrades Association)

A man and a woman stood on a lonely shore, with only the gentle lapping of the waves and the cries of the gulls for accompaniment. The man's thoughts were not in June 1977, but had transcended the dimension of time. He was again a young Troop Commander and his ears were not hearing the peaceful sounds of the present but a far more strident orchestra, and his eyes were again seeing those sights which had indelibly imprinted themselves on his memory at the same spot 34 years before. He gazed seawards and saw again the incredible vista of that vast armada filling the horizon, the like of which no man will ever see again. He remembered the landing craft of an earlier wave, lying broadside on to the shore, with a gaping hole in its side. He turned towards the land and his mind's eye saw again the crumpled battle-dress heaps on the sand, those young men whose short lives had ended on that day, only a few yards from the water's edge. In the dunes again there was the German gun crew, lying dead around their gun. He looked along the coast towards Arromanches, visible in the smoking haze, and saw not the quiet seaside town, but a place enveloped in the smoke and flashes of a bitter conflict where the killing was still going on through its narrow streets.

The whole scene seemed to him to be permeated with the aura of that lost generation, whose last day on earth had been 6th June 1944.

They had arrived in Arromanches the previous day, and after some brief conversation with the locals, the word got round about his earlier visit, and wherever they went, were treated like visiting royalty. The realisation dawned that in this part of Normandy, the French still respected 'Les Anglais'.

The visit to the Juin Museum was memorable to say the least. The lady curator insisted on conducting the tour in person and loaded the visitors with mementoes, having ushered them past the box office with a peremptory wave of dismissal to those who would have dared to ask payment for entry. They stood on the cliff tops near Arromanches, and looked at the remains of Mulberry still dotting the sea, and remembered the storm which partially wrecked it after only a few days of operation, recalling those traumatic days of sitting and taking what the Germans threw over, with our own artillery rationed to three shells per day. The pilgrimage continued from the beaches, inland over some of the same ground, and each name on signposts brought fresh waves of poignant memories. St. Gabriel, La Belle Epme, La Senaudiere. The crossroads at La Senaudiere, littered with burning Panthers and Shermans, almost looking down each other's gun barrels!

On to Tilly-sur-Seulles, probably the most evocative name of all. The last remembered sight of this – a booby-trapped ruin from end to end, and now not a trace of the former destruction, just another typical Normandy town, with only the roofs to give a clue – they all look new! Outside Tilly, a British Military Cemetery could not be passed without a visit, and after a long search, there they were – four graves in a row, all with the same date, and 61st Reconnaissance Regiment on the headstones. The sight of the names brought back the faces with clarity, and those of others in similar places from Normandy along that littered trail to the German border.

And so the pilgrimage ended, and the Troop Commander returned to the present and again thanked his lucky stars for being one of those fortunates who survived to tell the tale. A tale recalled so many times and remembered with gratitude and pride by the people of Arromanches.

Capt. A.R.V. Stone. MC.

> *Far other scene is Thrasimene now;*
> *Her lake a sheet of silver, and her plain*
> *Rent by no ravage save the gentle plough.....*

(Byron: Childe Harold's Pilgrimage: Canto IV)

Welcome to Max Murphy, 'B' Sqdn. Anti-tank, who writes:

Dear Friends,

Some years ago my wife and I attempted to retrace 'B' Sqdns route from the Normandy coast up into Holland and into the Ardennes. As I was having to rely solely on memory, no doubt we went off track a number of times but we did find a number of indications of 61st Recce's having been there. In the first place I searched for a familiar landscape on the Normandy coast slightly north of Arromanches and eventually I located a place that seemed to be the place that I had seen before us, as we stood offshore on the Liberty ship 'Fort Brunswick'. I suggested to my wife that we should take a certain route from the coast road and lo and behold there, as fresh as the day that they were painted, were the letters TT 41, in what looked like tar, on a house end. We overnighted in Bayeux and had a look at the Imperial War Graves Commission Cemetery there in which, sadly, we found a number of the graves of the lads who went over the Channel never to return. The graves are immaculately kept, though of little consolation to those who grieve.

The infamous Bois du Briquessard is now entirely cordoned off with barbed wire because of the vast quantity of unexploded shells and things that are still in there. It was interesting to see how twenty years of new growth had successfully eradicated most of the traces of our ever having been there.

Villers Bocage has been completely rebuilt and Falaise has undergone similar restoration. Tilly, Caumont and Conde show little signs of the tremendous battles that once raged around them….. Those involved in the crossing of the Albert Canal at Steelen will never forget that dreadful day – Friday I think. The bridge that was then blown has still not been fully repaired and there is a memorial in the local churchyard to record the day. In the lee of the church are yet more graves bearing the 61st Recce Regt. Insignia.

.Lomel has changed but little and the Journey up to Eindhoven does not take long when there are no Tiger tanks impending progress with their 88's. The town of Eindhoven has undergone a transformation and so has Nijmegam, though the bridge to the 'island' remains as ever. The people on the island were intrigued to learn that I had been there in the dark days and proved wonderfully hospitable, especially in the area around Driel……

Our travels took us through Arnhem, for the first time, and on into Germany down the Rhine as far as Mainz and then we doubled back so as to pass through the Ardennes. The little villages of Bure, Wellin, Tellin and Gripon are still pretty much as I remembered them, though there has been a certain amount of building work carried out. The Chateau de Wepion, midway between Dinant and Namur, where I spent Christmas 1944, is still there and seemingly unchanged.

In Iseghem, although I could no longer remember the name or the address of our hostess during the period when we were in 'civvy billets' there, I managed to find the house and to my surprise the same dear old lady was still in occupation. We had lunch with her and reminisced as best we could through the language barrier....... Trooper Harry Buxton and myself spent a few hours in the little village of Nederzwalm in 1944 waiting for the rest of you to catch up with us when we managed to get ourselves lost. Forlornly we sat on the steps of a little pub on a crossroads and one of the little girls of the village gave each of us a photograph of herself and her sister. For some reason or other I had kept the picture among my souvenirs and took it with me on the trip. I stopped at the pub to ask if they knew the recent whereabouts of the little girl. Imagine my surprise when the landlady said that *she* was the little girl! Incidentally, a couple of years ago, I saw a reader's letter in our local newspaper asking for first hand information on ghosts or apparitions. I jotted down an anecdote that had happened to a few of us in Trun, in Normandy. Eventually the anecdote appeared in the book 'Ghosts and Hauntings' by Dennis Bardens.

Yours sincerely

Max Murphy.

NORMANDY – 6TH JUNE 1969

(Newsletter Old Comrades Association)

An Account Of A Visit To Normandy By A Member Of Our Second Generation.

A more fitting appreciation of what the Normandy visit was all about could surely not have been better than by our youngest pilgrim, 14 year old Stephen Foot (son of Les), whose impressions, certainly shared by all, are movingly written in his letter which we are extremely pleased to reproduce below. Stephen writes:

I headed south towards Southampton just like the men before me who were going to land on the Normandy beaches 25 years previously on June 6th. Stopping on the way we picked up members of the 61st Recce. As they came on the coach though they were strangers, it seemed as if I had met them before, as my dad had told me about them.

I have never been abroad before so I was feeling excited anyway. But travelling through the Normandy countryside I imagined what it was like during those days in 1944 before I was born.

We arrived at our hotel in Caen and later took the coach to Bayeux. There at the cemetery, Colonel Mount and Colonel Brownrigg carried the wreath of flowers of the colours green and yellow, the Recce colours and we followed to see them lay it on the steps of the memorial. It was a very moving experience for me and I also felt very proud. It was there I saw many graves of the 61st and of the other Fallen. Some only a few years older than I am now. I am 14; some of the soldiers on the gravestones were only 18 when they were killed. Dying for me and others like me. I shall never forget it. Walking around the cemetery, leaving the graves in the grass and looking back and seeing them in the distance.

We visited Arromanche where we went into the museum, and I was interested in all the relics on display. Outside are several field guns.

Saturday night – the Reunion Dinner which was very good. I felt very privileged to be sitting down with the men who had fought 25 years ago. But I felt very sad when the toast after dinner was 'Absent Friends'.

I was given the map and the picture of the Recce badge by Mr Dawson. All the members of the party signed it for me. I have the map and badge hanging on my bedroom wall.

At Arromanche we found Gold Beach and the actual spot where the 61st had trundled up the beach. At Briquessard the lane leading up to the Allied positions still had old tins in the trenches not caved in by time. This seemed to be remarkable to me; still being there left by the men 25 years ago. And me, standing there where so many soldiers had been.

I found an old American water bottle, which thrilled me and I brought it home to keep as a souvenir. All around the area it was not hard to imagine the fighting. I realised again how much my generation owes to all those men who came to Normandy on June 6th 1944.

Some to stay forever. Some to return home disabled, and some like my father, lucky to be able to return and show me how it was for him when he was not much older than I am now.

Going to back to 'Leopard', crossing the English Channel again and coming back through England was very good, but very sad too.

I will never forget June 6th 1944, nor will I ever forget June 6th 1969 and all the people I met.

Stephen L Foot

(We understand Stephen is making the army his career and we all wish him happy comradeship as we enjoyed it in 61 Recce. Thank you for writing Stephen – it was a pleasure having you with us – and we won't remind too many that you came first in the race across Tancarville Bridge! ....Ed. TT41.)

SMILE FOR THE CAMERA

Dear Sir,

I detest formal clothes. I would never wear full evening dress. I think black jackets and striped trousers look ridiculous, and I just cannot see anything in a bowler hat.

'Push it further back, mate.'

MEMORIES – OLD AND NEW

NORMANDY & ARDENNES (PART 1) – 1990 BY ROY HOWARD 'A' SQDN

(Newsletter Old Comrades Association)

Roy and his two adult sons decided last year to make a 'Recce' to the continent and visit some of the places where the Recce Regiment saw action during the war. This is how the story goes. "The visit proved to be a most wonderful experience, especially having two sons for company. It was very much a return to those days of long ago in 1944 – three men in one modern but unarmoured A.R.C. and minus the hazards of enemy resistance. We managed to cover a lot of the old ground, exploring the full length of the Canadian and British landing grounds as far as the American Cemetery at Colleville-Sur-Mer and the German Cemetery at La Cambe. Then to Bayeaux Cemetery to pay our tribute to the 61st Recce dead.

By pure chance we also met Major John Howard at Pegasus Bridge discussing with Madame Condree-Pritchett the chances of saving the bridge from demolition in order to widen the road crossing. Then on to Jerusalem and Hottot-Le-Bagues and Villers Bocage. We also visited the Cemeteries at 'Ryes' and 'St Charles de Percy' where a number of 61st Recce also lie and was able to photograph the grave of Ernie Brobbin's friend Trooper Stevenson 10602554, killed on the 5th August 1944, one of many 1060 boys who lost their lives at such an early age.

Then on to the woods at Briquessard (there is another story about exploring the woods which can be mentioned later) – still some evidence of our occupation there, on to the Forest of L'Evaque, South of Caumont, then across France via Conde-sur-Noireau, Givet and into the Ardennes, through St Hubert to La Gleize. (The only surviving King Tiger Tank, still within 300 yards of where it ran out of fuel Dec '44).

Our final point was Malmady, then return via Hottot (more tributes left at War Cemetery to 61st Recce dead), and also at Tilly-Sur-Seulles Cemetery on behalf of the 61st Recce. Then on to Dinant and a mad dash to Toll AutoRoute from Valenciennnes via Rouen, Caen, Bayeaux to Ryes where we arrived at 3.00 am and slept until 8.30. A quick visit to the Museum of Peace at Caen and onto the 16.30 ferry Ouistreham to Portsmouth. Drove overnight back to Shrewsbury for 0.400 hrs on Saturday 16th. A distance by road of 1,700 miles since the 8th June. Exhausting – exhilarating and worth every minute."

(Roy Howard 'A' Sqdn)

Thank you Roy for such an interesting account of your trip.   *Ed. TT41.*

Roy has been making an extensive search to try and find information, which might lead to the identification of a Reconnaissance Corps Captain in the War Cemetery at Hottot-le-Bagues, Normandy. He has contacted the War Graves Commission, M.O.D. Public Records Office, and all other Recce Regts. Without success, but he is still trying and only time will tell.

NORMANDY & ARDENNES (PART 2) – 1990 BY ROY HOWARD 'A' SQDN

(Newsletter Old Comrades Association)

In addition to the War Cemeteries mentioned in the letter to Col. Brownrigg, we also visited the cemeteries at 'Ryes' and 'St. Charles de Percy' where a number of 61st Recce lie. We were able to photograph the grave of Ernie Brobbin's friend, Tpr. Stevenson 10602554, killed on the 5th August 1944, one of the many 1060 boys who lost their lives at such an early age.

It took a long time to explore the woods at Briquessard and find some evidence of our earlier occupation there. The area is mostly fenced off with notices to 'keep out' – Ministry of Defence warnings, but of course we translated these as an invitation to 'come in and explore'. We parked the car down a narrow forest track and crawled under the wire fence armed with a metal detector, which in fact proved to be quite useless. However, after a couple of hours – when I was certainly ready to give up, covered with tears and scratches from brambles and thorns and old pieces of barbed wire, we eventually found clear evidence of old slit trenches and mortar containers and the lid of a ration box bearing the magic date of 1944. (Super sleuth Howard strikes again!!!)

During our period in the woods, we saw a car, which stopped at the end of a track, and the driver must have been looking for us, because as soon as he spotted us, he took off in a hurry. Later, as we were talking to some of the locals in the village of Briquessard, the Gendarmarie arrived armed to the teeth and started to set up a roadblock on the road, which we had recently driven down. We thought no more of it at the time and we pushed on in the opposite direction heading for the Belgian border and the Ardennes.

On our return journey two days later, and in a hurry to get back to Caen for the ferry, the border was closed and cars were being allowed across with little delay until it came to our turn. We were ordered out of the car and escorted into the Customs Office by Belgian and French Police. Our pockets were emptied, and passports scrutinised. We were interrogated at great length, but none of the Police would respond to any English and our combined French was just not up to the standard needed to explain why three men should be mad enough to travel so many miles and sleep in a tent just for the fun of it.

We gave up any attempt after the point where we had tried to tell them about a Tiger Tank which we had found at La Gleize, and sat back to let them get on with it. As a parting joke I suggested that we were looking for la plume de ma tante, but I don't think this helped our cause a great deal.

We were held up for a good two hours while enquiries went on over the telephone to the immigration department, and even to the firm in Welshpool from which the boys had rented the car for our travels.

At last we were released and sent on our way with our passports stamped by both the Belgium and French Customs. (Must be quite unique in this day and age.) Before reaching the port at Caen, we were stopped three more times and all documents checked including driving licences and green card, but we were allowed on again after they had seen the stamps in our passport.

We even had problems at Portsmouth when we got back, and it was apparent that Customs had been given our registration number, because our car was the only one to be directed into the examination bay. Although Customs made us remove a lot of our luggage, they did not empty the whole lot and we were relieved that the metal detector (after proving to be useless), had been put underneath everything else. It could have been a bit of a problem explaining why we had taken it with us.

It wasn't until we reached home that we learned about the terrorist bomb explosion in Germany the previous day and the extensive hunt across several borders that we understood the significance of everyone's interest in us. Well it all added to the pleasures and the excitement of an exhausting but most enjoyable time.

(Roy Howard 'A' Sqdn)

'I am sure you will always remember this holiday Roy.'   *Ed. TT41.*

ACTION REPORT: - AT RYRE

(Newsletter Old Comrades Association)

Members will no doubt recall our announcement in 1970 TT41, of the death of (ex-Sgt.) Mr S J Atkins, MM, and the reference to the battle action in which he was involved at RYRE. Sgt Jim Timperley recalls association with Sgt Atkins and perhaps some of you recall where Jim left off:

'One afternoon, Captain (then Lieutenant) Payne–Ross and myself put two six pounder anti-tank guns in position on the left bank of the Escault Canal. Also on the right hand side of the bridge was one of our Bren Carriers. We went over the bridge to recce the land and came into a square. A young lady came up to us to say that her father would like to speak to us. We went into a Chateau and this gentleman – you could tell from the surroundings that he was a gentleman of the land – gave us a hearty welcome with drinks, saying that he was very pleased to see the English soldiers. We asked him if he had seen any Germans in the area, to which he replied that he had not. We came back over the bridge and informed Sgt Aktins of the information we had received but told him that we did not like the 'set-up' and to keep the lads on the alert. Leaving the rations for the teams, Lieutenant Payne-Ross and myself left for our HQ. Early next morning we heard what had happened at the bridge. On arriving at the Post I had a word with Sgt. Atkins and he told me that four enemy vehicles, two tanks and two troop carriers had come over the bridge, and, to his amazement the first vehicle had stopped, the other following suit. Then Sgt. Atkins had got another surprise. The Germans had got out of their vehicles and sat around smoking and talking. This is when Sgt. Atkins went into action. He shot at the third vehicle – a troop carrier, the other guns, i.e. the two six-pounders, opening up on the remainder. Sgt. Atkins, having apparently arranged that his firing would be the signal for the six-pounders also to open up. Sgt. Atkins said that bodies were flying all over the place and even up on to the telegraph wires. Sgt. Timperley concludes his account that this is what he recalls of the bridge at RYRE…..

Thanks for writing, Jim, - war-in-the-raw indeed.   *Ed.TT41.*

ACTION REPORT: - WITH 11TH ARMOURED DIVISION. JULY 31ST

(Newsletter Old Comrades Association)

The roads of Normandy were never really suitable for the movement of immense streams of traffic…. South of Caumont lay the real Bocage country. Earth banked fields and high hedges in twisting leafy lanes. It provided perfect cover for the defending Germans who were able to let us get right up to them before opening fire. Cases of ten or eleven armoured vehicles – tanks, half-tracks, and armoured cars could be instantly knocked out, and it happened with sickening regularity. As few as two Tiger Tanks could hold up an entire Armoured Brigade for hours. The 11th Armoured Division forced their way slowly forward, and in front of them the probing reconnaissance cars.

On the morning of July 31st, messages were coming back from the leading cars, often behind the enemy front, and sometimes, no messages at all – just silence from a particular car! Mixed up with these vital radio transmissions were lengthy instructions from Corps HQ, broken into now and again by some other vehicles trying to use the busy airwaves. At about 10.30 am a half-understood message was received at the rear from a leading car. The CO demanded an instant re-check, as the message seemed to be unbelievable. Back came the message again – "I say again, the bridge at 637436 is clear of enemy and still intact." This was the road over the river Sauleuvre six miles behind the German lines. It was being observed by one heavy and one light recce. car. The entire Corps Plan was altered and the advance of the 8th Armoured Brigade was switched to back up the lonely recce unit hiding in the woods. Only a single Frenchman knew they were there. He was the owner of a farm some 200 yds. from the bridge. What happened was that most of the leading vehicles had been blocked, one way or another, two cars were knocked out, and two cars made it over a crossroads before the German tank could get them too into its sights, and they moved flat out down a track through the forest of L'Eveque. Unknown at the time, this was the boundary between two German Divisions, each of which thought the other was holding it, and transport of both German Divisions were using it to withdraw from the Allied advance. The two recce cars found themselves travelling along in fast convoy for two miles with a German armoured car in front, and others following not far behind, all in a cloud of dust. Even if the Germans had recognised the British cars it is not likely that it would have made much difference. The German army was using some British equipment, including even Bren Carriers, captured four years ago at Dunkirk. When the genuine German vehicle turned up a side road, the two recce cars carried straight on and shortly after arrived at the bridge, crossed over, hid the cars in the wood, and leaving the radio operator to transmit the famous message went back on foot to keep observation on the bridge, spotted only by Monsieur Papillon, the farmer. They were only six men on their own with a radio set, six miles behind the German lines!

Lt. D.B. Powle, Troop Commander, was awarded the Military Cross for this operation.

(Roy Howard 'A' Sqdn.)

ADDENDUM – JUNE 1990

This Bridge apparently played a part of some importance, and last year a ceremony took place on the site and a plaque has been fixed on the bridge showing the Divisional sign of 11th Armoured Division, depicting a Bull. The bridge has now been named 'Le Pont du Taureau' with the date '31 Juillet, 1944.'

'Le Pont du Taureau 31 Juillet 1944'.

Roy Howard 'A' Sqdn stands guard once again over the same bridge 46 years later. (1990)

AND THEN THERE WERE THREE – AUGUST 4TH

Our Troop Sgt. Bill Abbey had been killed in an earlier patrol and had been replaced by our reserve Sgt. Joe Dunnington. Our Troop was (7Able) divided into two patrols, each patrol consisting of six in number, with two vehicles to each patrol. Patrol No.2 was sent to investigate a house from which radio masts could be seen. They drove to within 50 yards of the building without incident and the patrol commander – Sgt. Joe Dunnington decided to dismount and investigate on foot. Taking three men with him he cautiously entered the building whilst the rest of his patrol covered their approach and entry from the turrets of their two armoured cars. A few moments later there were explosions as he opened an interior door. The explosion left him critically wounded and the other two men rushed to his aid. A second explosion rang out and both his companions fell, severely injured. The three remaining members of the patrol left their vehicles and went to their aid without further problems. Sgt. Dunnington was bleeding to death from a severed artery in the groin. Trooper Ernest Brobbin gave each of the wounded an injection of morphine to relieve their pain. (Sgt. Dunnington died the following day.) Cpl. Ronnie Washburn had lost the side of his skull, exposing the brain, and Trooper Brobbin restrained the brain, inside the skull, with his hand, for over an hour until medics arrived, after a radio call for help. He survived but was severely handicapped throughout the rest of his life and his activities were restricted by damage to the brain and recurrent bouts of total memory loss.

He ended his days in a home run by the Royal British Legion. The third man – Trooper Bill Mathews had lost his right arm just below the shoulder and was evacuated to the UK after local surgery, in the nearest army General Hospital. Within minutes our troop strength had been reduced to nine men and we had to await the arrival of two N.C.O.'s and one trooper from reserves in Bayeaux, before the troop was brought back to strength.

I, as the only surviving N.C.O. was promoted to Troop Sgt. to replace Sgt. Dunnington and we had to learn to rely on the newcomers to settle in quickly to return to our previous operational efficiency.

(Roy Howard 'A' Sqdn.)

HOTTOT-LES-BAGUES WAR CEMETERY, CALVADOS, FRANCE (1990) GRAVE REF.IX.D.7.

4800261 SERGEANT
J. A. DUNNINGTON
61ST REGIMENT
RECCE. CORPS R.A.C.
5TH AUGUST 1944 AGE 29

EVER REMEMBERED BY ALL
AT MABLETHORPE

BARGAIN DAY IN BELGIUM

One day I received a visit from an American Captain who was looking for souvenirs. He was particularly interested in collecting enemy handguns and as I had picked up quite a number over the past few months he was anxious to relieve me of them. He was offering to swap an American Jeep for them and after a little haggling we came to an agreement. In addition to the Jeep, he agreed to throw in a Thompson sub-machine gun in exchange for five guns from my collection, and I handed over a P38 automatic, a 9mm Berreta, a Lugar Parabellum, a Mauser and a Webley .38 revolver. The American went off delighted with the deal, and it didn't take long to obliterate the original identification markings and to replace them with our own 'TT 41'.

I had to reach an agreement with our Troop Commander to share the use of the Jeep before he would agree to submit a formal request to H.Q. for the Jeep to be taken on to our vehicle strength, and we also had quite a problem persuading H.Q. to give two extra men to man the thing. It was all highly irregular and contrary to regulations, but we had long learned that regulations were there to be overcome.

At a later stage we managed to acquire a pair of Stirling Machine-guns from a crashed aircraft and these were soon mounted next to the driving seat. The Jeep proved to be great fun, and we used it quite effectively to reinforce our patrols. It proved to be its most effective during operations in the Ardennes, being so much lower in height than our normal vehicles we could drive beneath the low branches in the forest areas, and it was much easier to man-handle out of ditches when the ice proved to be a problem. We kept the Jeep until we were disbanded, and it was with great regret that I was unable to get it back to the UK. I sometimes wonder what price the Yanks placed on a Sherman tank?

(Roy Howard 'A' Sqdn.)

ACTION REPORT: - THE ESCAUT CANAL

61ST Recce. were holding a 35 mile front along the Escaut Canal from Ghent to Ouderarde. Our main activity was to keep up patrols along the front as we were stretched too thinly on the ground to hold all the bridges and cover any enemy crossings by boat. I was asked by two Royal Engineer Officers if I would try to recover their Jeep which they had driven up to the edge of the Canal and where they had abandoned it after coming under enemy fire. I took a light Recce Car up to a spot on the bank just below the Jeep, which was standing on the high part of an embankment at the approach to a demolished bridge. All appeared to be quiet so I started up the embankment on foot. Almost at the top I came under fire from a sniper and flung myself headlong down the bank. I then collected my own Heavy Recce Car and drove straight up the approach road until the opposite bank of the Canal was in full view. With head and shoulders above the turret top I examined the opposite bank carefully through binoculars and then directed my gunner to open up with the B.E.S.A. heavy machine gun on all windows of buildings visible across the water. The sniper took two more pot shots at me in retaliation, but I lowered myself into the turret as soon as I heard the shots strike the armoured plating. We then raked the Canal bank and gardens with the B.E.S.A. which brought a stronger reaction from the enemy who opened up with a 20mm: Oerlikon gun scoring two direct hits on our turret but with only minor damage. The muzzle flashes from the Oerlikon gave away its position amongst some trees and I ordered my gunner to change from B.E.S.A. fire to 37mm: cannon shells with high explosive charge. We fired about twenty rounds into the trees and saw the enemy gun crew scuttle for cover. Switching back to machine gun fire my gunner was able to eliminate them, but we failed to locate the persistent sniper. I then returned to patrol activity for the remainder of the day and returned to the spot after dark when we managed to recover the Jeep intact.

(Roy Howard 'A'Sqdn.)

ACTION REPORT: - ESCAULT CANAL

(Newsletter Old Comrades Association)

S.Q.M.S. Alf Wade now reveals hitherto unpublished facts to add to already written reports on this episode in September 1944. From the horse's mouth, so to speak, we quote:

We were crossing the canal at the crack of dawn with plenty of 'fireworks' around, and had reached midstream on the Assault Bailey Bridge, when my driver, Trooper Box let out a yell and said, "I've been shot!" My reply was unprintable! However, he had been shot – in the knee - and without more ado he slammed on the brakes and dived out of the cab. I sat there like a lemon. Then realising our predicament I leapt out of the cab (narrowly avoiding jumping straight into the canal) and ran round the front of the truck to see Trooper Box crawling as fast as his one sound fat hairy leg could propel him back to the 'safe' side of the bridge. Tony Anthony, my cook and past master at lobbing out short rations, had been rudely awakened from his slumbers, and had jumped out from the rear of the truck. I yelled at him to grab 'Box' and get him off the bridge. Then I jumped into the cab whereupon a machine gunner opened up, and to my horror put a burst within inches of my head, making a hole in the roof as easily as a G1098 tin-opener. It seemed ages before I got the engine started and moved slowly off the bridge with my head in a hull-down position. On reaching the other side and the cover of a farm building I met Harry Rolfe and saw the funny side of the story from his point of view.

Harry Rolfe was shown a copy of Alf's letter, and replied, "It made very good reading for me and clarified certain points that I was hazy about. But certainly did not know that Trooper Box had been wounded in the knee. It was good of Alf to amplify the incident."

Alf continues to reminisce on that black day for 'C' Squadron........Was the brewing of a large bowl of char to steady the nerves. I walked around the area to see if there were any takers and rounding a bend in the road came across one of our young '1060' boys from 15 or 16 Troop who was staggering back with a serious injury to his lower jaw. The problem was to try and feed him some tea.... Someone had a brainwave, by using a farmhouse straw, enabling him to suck some of our warm sweet tea. A very brave lad (either Arthur Broughton or Cecil Wackett will know his name), and I believe the 'Medics' were able to fit him with a silver lower jaw and generally made an excellent job of what had been an indescribable sight."

Thanks for writing Alf – another reminder of the suffering behind the victory.　　*Ed.TT41.*

ACTION REPORT: - FROM ERIC POSTLES 'B' SQUADRON

(Newsletter Old Comrades Association)

"Of the three carrier crews, two were lost: Bill Griffiths, Joe Collier, Jack Webb and Jock McHugh died on the Sunday morning after D-Day when they ran over a massive mine, shortly before, Sammy Benson was wounded. The other crew died when we were entering 'harbour' during the 'swan' in Northern France. Here we lost Digger Day, Jock Buchan, another trooper from Yorkshire and Lieutenant Soul was badly wounded. We thought that the weight of prisoners we had on each carrier had exploded a mine in one of our own panniers. Shortly afterwards, 10 Troop was involved in the action at Eine. Burt Mopham and I were on 'stag' before stand–to when the Germans arrived. I roused the anti-tank crew and well remember the panic when the firing mechanism which had been removed the previous day during the celebrations with the locals, could not be found. Luckily it was, and Wally Grant was able to deal effectively with some of the enemy vehicles."

N.B. Eric Postles served 43 years with the Civil Service after the war, and in November 1984 he was made a Companion of the Imperial Service Order, which he received, from H.M. the Queen at Buckingham Palace.

SMILE FOR THE CAMERA

Michael helped the old lady with her luggage up three flights of stairs.
Do you smoke? She asked.
Yes, thanks I do.
Thought so, said the lady, you're well out of breath for your age...

ACTION REPORT: - ESCAULT CANAL

(Newsletter Old Comrades Association)

Reports continue to pour in of the Battle Action – but whilst it has been referred to as the Escault, it would appear in fact that the action was perhaps on the Albert Canal...?

If I'd known what was going to happen on that particular day in September 1944, I don't think that I'd have bothered to get up!

As it was, we were roused at some unearthly hour (about 3.30 am) and told to move out. It was bitterly cold and we'd no idea where we were going or why. Normally I rode in the half-track of B Troop (HQ Sqdn) with Lt Johnny Heitman and its driver Tommy Adams. Being perished however I decided to ride up front in a Chevy 15cwt with Len Lambert. The Chevies had a little door through to the engine that allowed the heat to come back.

Eventually after a fairly long ride we left the main highway and turned left into a small village –Stelen – there was an officer standing at the fork of the road in the village directing 'soft' vehicles straight ahead and 'hard' vehicles into some reserve area to the left. We passed the village church on our right and followed a rough earth track to the bank of a canal. Neither Len Lambert nor I had the foggiest idea where we were, we simply followed the other trucks. Over on our right we could make out the shattered outlines of a blown bridge and in front of us some geezer frantically waving his arms for us to advance. Up to that point it had been a fairly normal journey, but then we found the Chevy poised high atop the bank of the canal and a precipitous drop to a somewhat frail looking pontoon bridge across the canal itself. The canal wasn't all that wide and over on the far side was a small red brick farm building. It was just to the right of the roadway on the far side of the bridge. Len dropped into bottom gear and we semi-slid down the bank and onto the pontoon bridge. At that moment all hell was let loose. Bullets came tearing into the cab and body of the truck and I was actually aware of some cheeky bod in a coal scuttle helmet potting at us with a pistol from the shelter of the red brick building. We were powerless to do anything about it. Len's Sten gun was in the back of the truck, and my rifle was in the half-track, wherever that was. One bullet tore the heel off Len's right boot but we somehow managed to get safely up the other bank and off the road into a field. Water was pouring out of the radiator, a fan blade had been knocked off and the carburettor damaged. Other shots had gone through the back of the truck and some had even gone through some boxes of 6-pounder ammunition without doing any particular damage. I can't remember what Len Lambert did, but I know I headed for a convenient ditch and found it occupied by an infantry Sergeant (DLI) who'd had his knee shattered. Someone further up the ditch said there was a Regimental Aid Post in a nearby farm building, so I helped the Sergeant to get there. Realising that he had got himself a 'Blighty' he promptly made me a present of a German P38 pistol and some ammunition and I headed back to the ditch feeling a little braver now I was armed. As I looked back across the bridge I could see Sewell descending the far bank with his water truck. I can only think that our Teutonic opponents thought it was a petrol bowser, because they pelted it with everything they had. When Sewell, looking badly shaken, got to our side of the canal, water was pouring from a myriad of holes in the tank. Fine for keeping down the dust on the roads, but dust was the least of our problems that day.

Not having any clear directions from anyone as to what to do, I headed over to the Aid Post to see what was happening over there. They were extremely busy with casualties from a number of units involved in the action and coping very well indeed despite the airbursts banging away every few seconds.

I remember that 'Smudger' Smith, Sergeant HQ B Troop Anti-Tank, decided to get out of the cold and into Len Lambert's Chevy parked in the field. He wrapped a blanket round himself and settled down in the passenger seat for a kip. He hadn't been there a few minutes when an 88-mm air burst enveloped the truck in smoke. I thought Smithy was a goner for sure, but out through the smoke ran a blanket with Smithy in it. The blanket was riddled with holes, as was the cab, but Smudger himself suffered nary a scratch. I saw a laddie with serious jaw injuries coming to the Aid Post, I remember him trying to put his tin hat on – then someone knocked it out of his hand. I seem to remember someone saying he was a carrier driver and the damage to his jaw was done by a 20 mm Oerliken shell. It seems the Germans were using these anti-aircraft weapons against the carriers. The rest of the day I remember very little about, except confusion everywhere and somebody said some enemy wounded were in a ditch that ran parallel to the canal. A couple of us went to look. No actual dead or wounded, but we did find a Spandau…. It was early evening when I went back over the bridge to Stelen. I found Johnny Heitman, Tommy Adams, Harry Buxton and some of the other fellows in a café. Just as I arrived so did Captain Hugh Thorne (our battery commander). He had the mail with a letter for me. I recognised the handwriting. It was from my girlfriend – a 'Dear John' telling me that she was going to marry some munitions worker. I should have known it was going to be 'one of those days.' We ate and decided to kip down where we were for the night. I found myself on the café billiard table and pretty soon fell asleep, only to be awakened by an 88 mm shell hitting the café. The Germans mounted a counter attack and it seemed expedient that we should retire to a safer position. When we went out of the café, we found Harry Buxton's motor bike hanging from the spiked churchyard railings where the shell blast had lodged it. The remainder of the night we spent in another café two or three km away.

61 Recce lost several men in that particular action some of them are still buried in the churchyard at Stelen. The people of the village have erected a memorial to the TT Division in the churchyard. The café has been rebuilt and the same people still own it. The road leading up to the pontoon bridge is still there. The red brick building and the building of the Aid Post are still there, but the atmosphere is such that no-one would ever believe battle had ever been joined in that quiet little part of Belgium.

Max Murphy

N.B. An annual ceremony is held at the memorial in that churchyard to commemorate.

ACTION REPORT: - ALBERT CANAL AREA

(Newsletter Old Comrades Association)

Foreign Correspondent Pete Hussey, was hanging 'Around the Squadrons' when it was decided to pull him out of the queue to tell us about his globe-trotting Wicker's World, and first of all here Pete and Glad are in Aplnachstad, Switzerland – with two Swiss friends, walks 20 miles in two days, sleeping in a hay barn at 7,000 feet. If that's what relegation of Oxford United does for you… Gladys stayed at Alpach – we were a bit worried in case the strain of carrying the three haversacks made her feet ache.

Next we were in Ballymena visiting Glad's relations. Look-see at Cromore Camp and Cromore (Portstewart) Halt (deserted). Then whip down to Portrush. The café has gone, and of the Battalion HQ area the houses are still there although shops now occupy ground level. Actually this trip was undertaken in '75 and Pete took several photographs, which are exhibited at reunions.

Back to '76 and Pete and Glad on another visit to Izegem, where a Belgium friend from Tielt took them to Gheel and Stelen. The Albert Canal is now a very wide waterway, and the ends of the old 1944 bridge are gone. A visit to Stelen church where the graves were well kept and where are buried 61 Recce's 5337851 L/Sgt S Smith, age 26 years; Trooper R Robinson age 25 years and 5676900 Trooper A E Matthews age 28 years: the remaining graves are those of the Durham Light Infantry. Facing the churchyard is a large new notice:

'On the 8th, September 1944 began from here the Battle for Geel by
50th Northumbrian Division.'

There is only one pre-war house in Stelen. In talking to the old lady who happened to be outside sweeping the front, she said that her house is the only old house left. She remembers German snipers in the church steeple across the road. The café has now changed hands and new people there. Pete asked her about the group of houses which 14 Troop attacked with the Carriers under Lt Spilsbury, the lady pointed over to one old red brick house on the right over the new bridge on the Geel road: the only house left of that group that we attacked in the face of 20mm and Spandau fire, and where Jerry loped off in the direction of Geel to later mortar us very accurately for our trouble and after that, counter attack with tanks which ended up with Lt Spilsbury and Pete in hospital and Pete's discharge a couple of weeks before the war ended.

DISCOMFORTS & TRIBULATIONS

We learned to accept the dangers and the risks of our activities without complaint. We did the same too as far as discomfort was concerned, but for some reason it was the discomfort, which we found to be the greater hardship. Our rations consisted entirely of 'Compo' packs. These were lightweight wooden crates, each containing rations for six men for a three-day period. The contents varied little, but the favourites contained bully beef or Spam, rather than the alternatives of stew or oxtail and haricot. All packs contained greengage jam, cheese, greasy bacon, powdered milk, powdered egg, salt, sugar, hard tack biscuits, boiled sweets, cigarettes, matches and three pieces of very rough toilet paper per man. Our habits were not expected to be regular or frequent! The rations were quite good, and we soon learned to crush the 'dog-biscuits' into pieces with the aid of a heavy instrument, and add them to a stew. We were seldom short of a brew up at any time and at every opportunity, but we never saw a slice of bread, and it is surprising how often we spoke about this missing luxury. Those who did not smoke swapped their fags for boiled sweets, and the fag ration kept most men happy. We also received regular supplies of Benzedrine tablets to enable us to remain awake for up to 56 hours at a time. Sleep was one of the things we really missed out on. Our usual routine was to return each night to harbour in the cover of some woodland before darkness fell. Here we hid up until the next day's patrols. The days throughout June and July were very long, starting at 4.45 am and dusk not falling until 11.15 pm. When we reached our nightly harbours after the day's events, our first task was to dig slit trenches for protection against mortar or artillery fire. The vehicles each had to be refuelled, ammunition replaced, guns cleaned, and vehicle maintenance carried out before preparing our own food. One man, usually the driver dealt with the food, while the gunner/radio operator cleaned and oiled the guns and stood by to tune in to a new radio frequency for tomorrow's operation. Every man took up a defensive position around the harbour in case of infantry attack, and this 'stand-to' was maintained for one hour after sunset and again for one hour before dawn. The day's work started therefore at 3.45 am, and finished at 15 minutes after midnight. Between these few hours each troop of 12 men took it in turn each night to provide sentries until the dawn stand-to. After the evening stand-to an 'Order Group' was held for Officers and Troop Sergeants who gathered with the CO to receive their orders for the next days operations. They then returned to their own Troop to brief crews and mark up maps from the references given out at the 'O' Group. We also used codes when referring to map references over the radio, and these codes, in Slidex formulations were changed daily. We were also given new identification call signs for each vehicle for radio communication between each patrol. Known or suspected enemy positions were marked up on each vehicle commander's map using coloured chinagraph pencils. There was never enough sleep for anyone, and in spite of the help given by Benzedrine tablets, lack of sleep was as deadly as enemy ambush. What little sleep we did get, we took at the bottom of our slit trenches come rain, hail, and snow. We also found the flies and wasps a great burden. The flies were enormous, spending all day feeding on the blood of dead British and German alike, and on the bloated corpses of the many dead cattle lying in the fields and farmyards. Another indescribable abomination, was the stench given off by these bodies. It wasn't just putrefaction or decay, they became swollen and bloated with gas gangrene, and as they disintegrated they filled the air with their stench which was inescapable. The final hardship perhaps, was doing without a bath. It was four months before any of us had an opportunity to fully undress, and of course, we were unable even to remove our boots at night.

Eventually we were able to pay a flying visit to an army shower unit, set up in a field by the Royal Engineers Hygiene Unit. We visited it once only, a small collection of canvas waist-high screens under the open sky, and a moderate trickle of luke-warm water containing something like Jeye's fluid disinfectant.

Roll on bath time at home!

(Roy Howard 'A'Sqdn.)

SMILE FOR THE CAMERA

A Pete Hussey special is the one about a Sergeant and a Private being charged for kicking the RSM. The Sergeant said he tripped accidentally, and was acquitted. Said the Private: "Well, I saw the Sergeant kick the RSM and thought the war must be over!" He got 28 days detention.

UTRECHT – HOLLAND – ERNEST BROBBIN 'A' SQDN.

(Newsletter Old Comrades Association)

In one of Ernest's letters, he mentioned that back in 1944 'A' Sqdn. Stopped for a short period near Utrecht just long enough to get out his "Barbers kit" to cut some of 7, 7A, 8 and 8A troop's hair including Major Chapman who he said paid him. It wasn't in a Barber's chair, but sitting on the grass verge by some Victorian -type houses.

While this operation was taking place, a lady from one of these houses came over to Ernest and asked him if he was a professional hairdresser, to which he replied "No". She then asked if he would be kind enough to cut her father's hair – what could he say – the father was 80 years old with long white hair on his shoulders wearing a pill box hat and had never had it cut since the German occupation. His reward was sticks of shaving soap and cakes – what more could you ask for. He found out later that the father was a Scotsman married to a Dutch lady who had since died, and his two daughters spoke perfect English.

SMILE FOR THE CAMERA

'HEALTH WARNINGS'

WORK	-	*Can wear you out.*
EATING	-	*Can make you fat.*
SMOKING	-	*Can give you cancer.*
DRINK	-	*Can ruin your liver.*
TV	-	*Can ruin your eyes.*
NOISE	-	*Can make you deaf.*
SEX	-	*Can give you aids.*
CARS	-	*Can kill.*
WAR	-	*Can stunt your growth.*
So, what's left?	-	*Go back to ruddy sleep!*

TOURNAI: - REMEMBERED

(Newsletter Old Comrades Association)

A true experience recalled by Mr. 'Posh' Price. HQ Mortars (A memory too for Cpl. Jack Cowley and perhaps others, present at the time).

1944 – a lone M/c rider as I entered Tournai to be stopped by two gendarmes. After looking at my shoulder flash (Reconnaissance) they asked me what French Regiment did I belong to. When I told them that I and my comrades behind were English, they gave a signal and, to my profound astonishment, some four to five hundred people, carrying Union Jacks and flowers, appeared from nowhere and surrounded me.

At a given signal, a lane parted and an elderly gentleman with a beautiful girl on his arm, walked down toward me. She opened her arms, placed them round me and said with tears in her eyes, but with a lovely smile, "I kiss the first English soldier to enter our town" and being a perfect gentleman, I said to her "Okay by me love, get cracking" which she did, bless her.

I was then asked if I could bring my comrades back with me. I said that I would try. I was then taken across a railway level crossing facing steps leading to a large building from which a Lady Superior, some nurses and an untold multitude of youngsters, all waving small Union Jacks and cheering, appeared. The Lady Superior came to me, blessed me and one young nurse ran to me crying, with a letter in her hand, asking if I could get it back to England for her to her people who had not heard from her for four years as she had been caught and trapped there by the speed of the German advance. I said yes, I would – and I did, by kind permission of Major Alexander. Having promised to do my best to bring my comrades back with me if I could, the most kissed Sergeant in the world returned to base.

I believe it was the assault officer, although not sure of his name, who said yes, he would come with his Troop and the Mortar Section as well. Back to Tournai we went amid tumultuous cheering, where they singled me out and stood me on top of a car, with an interpreter to speak to the crowd. I laid it on thick, praising them for their courage under the German yoke. The cheers were indescribable for they were made with delight. Then the Officer and several others were taken into a building (like a Town Hall) where they produced a beautifully bound book on the front of which, was inscribed in printed bold letters 'The Liberation Book.' The date was inserted and several of us, including myself, signed it. Then an amazing thing happened as we went outside.

The crowd opened into two lanes leading to the cemetery into which we followed the men. Here they stopped by a flower-topped well-tended grave. The spokesman looked at it and in the silence, which had now descended upon the gathering, loudly addressed it with the words: "My friend, you can now rest in peace. Your English friends are here as we promised you they would some day. You were badly wounded and we hid you from the Germans, nursed you as best we could but you died. We have kept our promise to you and so rest in peace."

N.B. In 1944 after being wounded behind enemy lines, Mr 'Posh' Price was evacuated to the UK by air in a Dakota of the RAF Transport Command, he had been involved in the action at the Albert Bridge.

OPERATION MARKET GARDEN
(ARNHEM) SEPTEMBER 1944

The Corridor – Belgian Border to Arnhem

XXX Corps commanded by General Sir Brian Horrocks, consisted of the Guards Armoured Division, 50th (TT) Infantry Division and 43rd Infantry Division 8th Armoured Brigade, and the Royal Netherlands Brigade amounting to a force of some 20,000 vehicles – armoured cars, tanks, trucks, transporters, guns etc. Obstacles on the route included nine waterways: three major rivers, ranging from 200 to 400 yds wide, the Maas, the Waal, and the Nedr Rijn; three small rivers, the Upper and Lower Dommel and the Aa; and three major canals, the Wilhelmina, the Willems, and the Maas-Waal. These waterways would confine the motorised column to the road for most of the way, a distance of approximately 65 miles. The two infantry divisions had suffered heavy losses in Normandy and there were no more reinforcements available. (One other infantry division had already been broken up in order to bring the other divisions up to strength.)

Sunday 17th September:
The advance was led by the Irish guards of the Guards Armoured Division, with 50th (TT) Division – already holding the line in front – to move and cover the flanks of the Armoured Division as it crossed the start line at 14.35 hours. The first stretch of ground was marshy, and the next was thickly wooded. Infantry and armour of 50th (TT) Division were to do what they could on either side of the road……. In two minutes, nine tanks went up in flames and the half-mile of roadway was littered with their burning wrecks. As the survivors leapt from their turrets they were cut down by enemy small-arms fire. Within the next hour Typhoons of the RAF flew 230 sorties in support of the Guards. By 17.30 hours: they reached the bridge just outside Valkenswaard and entered the town just after dark. General Horrocks had hoped to reach Eindhoven on the first day, but the airborne timings had shortened the day from 24 hours to 10 and the opposition had proved to be much stronger than anticipated.

Monday 18th September:
As soon as the mists cleared, armoured cars were sent out far ahead to reconnoitre routes for the tanks – North to Eindhoven and East towards Leende, Geldrop and Helmond, while the infantry of 50th Division held off bridgehead attacks and the Household Cavalry moved out of Volkenswaard and linked up with the US 101st Airborne Division at Woensel, North of Eindhoven. The bridge at Son was blown by the Germans and all that got across was one troop of armoured cars.

Tuesday 19th September:
The canal at Son was bridged and crossed at 06.15 hours and XXX Corps linked up with the American Airborne at Grave.

Wednesday 20th September:
The enemy twice severed the lifeline of XXX Corps' advance between Uden and Veghel on the 22nd and 24 hours later at St Oedenarde. The 50th (TT) Division was diverted to assist the 101st US Airborne in driving off the enemy, and by late into the day of 26th September the road was re-opened. The fifteen-mile stretch of road between Eindhoven and Veghel was to become known as 'Hells Highway'. Meanwhile the US 82nd Airborne Division had dropped and were holding the bridge at Nijmegen after four unsuccessful assaults, until the fifth, and successful attack on the 20th September backed by tanks of the Guards Armoured Division.

Monday 25th September:
By that evening it was decided to withdraw the survivors of the 1st British Airborne from the North bank of the Neder Rijn at Arnhem, and under cover of night and driving rain, about 2,300 of the original 10,000 who had fought North of the river came back.

Casualties:
Total British casualties were over 13,000. Casualties of Polish and Glider Pilots were 7,578. XXX Corps lost 1,480. V111 & X11 British Corps lost another 3,874.

61st Recce leaving 'THE ISLAND' in floods (November 1944)

Photo: - From 'This Band of Brothers.'(Jeremy Taylor)
'Towrope' (Capt. Joe Meredith) leading R.H.Q.

NIJMEGEN – 26TH SEPTEMBER 1944

By way of the re-opened corridor, the 50th (Northumbrian) Division of General D. Graham now also begins to enter the Nijmegen area from the south. This column of Humber Mk.IV armoured cars of the 61st Recce Regiment in Sint-Annastraat on its way to Keizer Karelplein and will continue to Overbetuwe via the Waal Bridge. The circle left on the cupola identifies this car as belonging to the C-Squadron. The TT sign on the mudguard stands for 'Tyne and Tees', another name for the Northumbrian Division.

By evening the 'seaborne tail' of Gavin's division also arrives at the Maas Bridge in Grave. Each unit of the 82nd has a guide waiting at the bridge, to conduct every section as quickly as possible through the darkness to its own unit at the front. There the seabornes, and no less their supplies, are welcomed with cheers.

The 61st Recce Regiment in Sint-Annastraat - HOLLAND

BOOK REVIEWS

REMEMBER ARNHEM - BY JOHN FAIRLEY

(Newsletter Old Comrades Association)

The story of the 1st Airborne Reconnaissance Squadron at Arnhem and sold in aid of the Airborne Forces Security Fund.

The Squadron was a unique small unit seeing active service in North Africa, Europe and Norway, and its story and individuals who served in its ranks are graphically described.

With an accurate and well balanced report of the 1st Airborne Division in Holland in September 1944 as background, the greater part of the story tells of the battle of Arnhem through the activities and involvement of the Officers and men of the Recce Squadron as told by surviving members – hundred or more found – and related to the documentary material available in the Public Records Office and elsewhere.

Whilst a tale of ordinary men from the totality of it all, there emerges something that is truly extraordinary, for the sum of their collective experiences is unquestionably one in which the qualities of comradeship, fortitude, humour and ingenuity are mystically combined and interwoven into an astonishing story of human courage and endurance. This was the real Arnhem.

In his foreword, Major General Urquhart, one time Commander of 1st Airborne Division, writes that future historians may well be grateful to John Fairley for this excellent result of persistent work.

The book consists of c.240 pages, 16 plates and 11 maps. If any difficulty in obtaining please contact publishers: Pegasus Journal, Browning Barracks, Aldershot GU11 2BS.

(We would like to thank John Fairley for his interesting letter, and we had pleasure in meeting at 49th and 56th Recce Reunions, and hope he will join us with perhaps friends of the unit, in April '79). *Ed. TT41*

ONLY THE ENEMY IN FRONT - BY RICHARD DOHERTY

The Recce Corps at War 1940 - 1946

(Newsletter Old Comrades Association)

Only the Enemy in Front (the title is taken from the unofficial motto of the Recce Corps) is the first comprehensive history of this spearhead fighting Corps formed in 1941 to replace the divisional cavalry regiments which had traditionally performed this role but which were transferred to the Royal Armoured Corps after Dunkirk.

The standard reconnaissance battalion carried twice as much firepower as its infantry counterpart: it was designed to move quickly in armoured recce cars, universal carriers and trucks: and it was to send its information back by wireless. Sir Arthur Bryant summarised the role as 'that of the cat's whiskers – armoured, mechanised transmitting whiskers. Those who served had to be intelligent, enterprising, brave, enduring and highly skilled.'

Using a combination of War Diaries, personal reminiscences and published material Richard Doherty – author of a number of military books – tells the stories of all the reconnaissance regiments that saw active service. All the important theatres of war and battles are represented here: Singapore (where the Corps first saw action): Egypt and the Western Desert: Tunisia: Sicily: Italy: Burma (including one regiment with Wingate's Chindits): North-West Europe (which includes a squadron at Arnhem) through to Germany.

Starting with a study of the background and formation of the Corps as a result of the deliberations of the Bartholomew Committee in June 1940, Only the Enemy… looks at the early days, the need to improvise in equipment and training, the lack of understanding among divisional commanders of the role of a recce battalion, and even the quest for a cap badge for the Corps.

Throughout the book the theme of the importance of reconnaissance is developed and the unique ethos of the Corps that made them an elite force in their day is given due credit. Many actions are covered in some detail to illustrate the special nature of the work of a reconnaissance regiment in the field.

Publication Date - 14 July 1994

Tom Donovan Publishing Ltd
52 Willow Road
Hampstead
London NW3 1TP

LIGHT-HEARTED ACCOUNT OF SERIOUS MATTERS

(Newsletter Old Comrades Association)

Squadrons came and squadrons went but RHQ went on forever – or so it seemed to the stalwarts of RHQ on the damp dreary and dismal 'ISLAND', that notorious place between Nijmegen and Arnhem we got to know so well during that October/November '44. But perhaps it was not all bad with its lighter moments and occasional light relief – the writer coming to rest on his ass at the feet of RSM Lunn, having parted company with a BSA M20 on a well known greasy drive. With a bright 'Morning Sir' pushed it away to straighten footrest and gear change lever – by heck, Mr RSM did manage a faint smile… Then there was the occasional appearance of 'Towrope' Joe Meredith with the NAAFI truck ably supported perhaps by Bill Stockford and Jock Daigh, his opening gambit puffing smoke from his pipe – 'Sorry Corporal, no pipe tobacco. Stuff it with Woodbines; we have plenty of bootlaces, blanco, brasso etc!' So I settled for toothpaste. Then the occasion when the writer deciding that a real bath would be very welcome, and having heard that such things were possible back in Nijmegen where HQ Squadron then had their feet under the table in civvy billets, arranged this happy event. On putting it into operation however, taking a truck to HQ for exchange or some such pretext, encountered the aforementioned 'Towrope' (no time to dodge) 'What are you doing here Corporal?' – Self, taking bull by the horns, 'bringing truck x and getting a bath at the same time sir'… 'Get back where you belong!' North it was again, over Nijmegan bridge where, as Colonel Brownrigg wrote the heart sank everytime you did it, and in my memory the throttle foot also went down hard on many occasions……..Then the night we had a prisoner. I was Guard Commander, doing my rounds when I encountered the sentry who had 'found' this person. In the pitch black of the Island, illuminated intermittently by a firework or two over towards Arnhem, it was difficult to see who or what we had. The nearest source of light was the Intelligence Office so there we took him. Opening the door, we shoved him in, to be confronted by a bemused IO Colonel Brownrigg, and Sgt Cotter. We then divested this disreputable figure of various knives, pistols and what have you, which were in his pockets, socks and anywhere else. The Intelligentsia questioning him did not get very far, the odd grunt as I remember. It turned out eventually that he was an American deserter…….. Oh, the excitement of it all!…… Just a couple of episodes which come immediately to mind – except perhaps Claude Howes and George Harries demonstrating how a m/c should be ridden under adverse conditions – suffering the same fate as I earlier! The occasional hogbaiting foray of course – but participants will remember………. And so it was, with hubs awash, to Iseghem and thought of civvy Christmas dinner – to which Von Rundstedt put paid, and away we went again…… the Ardennes: Captain Chapman receiving a snowball in his Jeep and rollicking me for laughing – but it was nothing to do with me sir – it whistled past my ear from behind and obviously aimed at the back of my head…… still in the Ardennes, I distinctly remember aircraft with no propellers over a river crossing towards the end of the campaign – first operational jets? And the sight of Lt Sprague on a horse is well recorded……….. So back to Iseghem (too late for Christmas) – and I went off to join 3rd Recce and Wessel and stations East.

Reg Harper RHQ

OPERATION MARKET GARDEN

U.S. CASUALTIES

Glider pilots and 9th Troop Carrier Command, were 3,974.

82nd Airborne Division – 1,432.

101st Airborne Division – 2,118.

GERMAN LOSSES

In Arnhem itself – 3,300

Along the 'Corridor' – nearly 10,000 more.

Owing to manpower shortages in the British 2nd Army, US 82nd and 101st Airborne Divisions were moved north of the Waal to the 'ISLAND' to hold the tip of the salient with 61st Reconnaissance Regiment; and remained there until the end of November. In this period their losses equalled those taken during the Airborne phase. They became a much blooded Division before returning to Reims for a well earned rest, and within three weeks, they and the 61st Reconnaissance Regiment were fighting alongside each other again in the Ardennes.

(Account as recorded in 'March to Victory' and 'Race for the Rhine Bridges'.)

(Roy Howard 'A' Sqdn.)

ICE & WHISKY - (CHRISTMAS DAY 1944)

The day was spent on the top of a mountain near Dinant. Temperature was the lowest recorded for sixty years. Engines had to run every twenty minutes to ensure their continual operation. The traversing mechanism of the turret froze solid and ice had to be chipped from hatches and access door. One man lost the skin from the palm of his hand on touching the bare metal without gloves. Dressed in white camouflage overalls, we crouched in holes dug in the snow and watched our German opponents moving now and again in the valley below us. There was little activity other than an exchange of sniper fire at irregular intervals. The Troop Commander and myself had each received a bottle of whisky from the Officer's and Sergeant's mess which had reached us on Christmas Eve, and to mark the occasion we shared our treasures with the rest of the Troop, drinking the lot by adding it to boiling hot 'compo' tea with no milk but plenty of sugar. We remained in our positions throughout the day and hoped that we would not be called upon to mount up and attempt to move on the icy mountain roads. In the still mountain air we heard our enemy doing their best to raise their spirits with an occasional Christmas Carol, and both sides did their best to avoid challenging each other. When darkness fell we settled down to a cold sleepless night, and wondered how much longer the war would last. On boxing day, fighting started again and we moved forward under an artillery barrage to take over the position held yesterday by our German neighbours who had received a morning visit from the RAF rocket firing Typhoons.

Peace and Goodwill was at an end.

NB: During the Ardennes operations we lost another 45 of our number, including another personal friend, Cpl Dennis Dolby, who smashed into the rear of an armoured vehicle on his motor cycle, and whose eyesight was severely damaged.

(Roy Howard 'A'Sqdn.)

ACTION REPORT - THE AFFAIR IN THE ARDENNES

(Newsletter Old Comrades Association)

By the morning of January 3rd 1945, the weather had become our worst enemy. We attacked on this day in a driving blizzard. Snow was falling continuously and the roads were ice-bound. Consequently, little progress was made, although the 6th Armoured Division reached the outskirts of Bure where the 13th Parachute Battalion and the 3rd Royal Tank Regiment became engaged in heavy fighting. Further North, at Wavreille, the 7th Parachute Battalion gained a footing in the town. The approaches to Wavreille were reconnoitred by two Troops of the 61st Reconnaissance Regiment: under the command of Lt M A Urban-Smith and Lt W Fling. They had with them a section of the Belgian Special Air Service mounted in Jeeps and bristling with machine guns. This section was commanded by a Sgt who was a Belgian nobleman and who owned most of the land over which we were operating. Consequently, he was most anxious to assist in the expulsion of the Huns. Halfway to their objective they spotted some Germans coming up behind. They quickly opened fire and those who survived surrendered. Slogging on through snow and sleet, they reached the outskirts of Wavreille and immediately became violently engaged with the enemy. Aided by the Belgians, they drove the enemy from the village but were counter-attacked strongly and it became necessary to withdraw. The following day the 7th Parachute Battalion and the 2nd Fife and Forfar Yeomanry joined to attack the village of Wavreille again. The tanks advanced across the open ground, firing as they went and the paratroops sprinted from position to position. Casualties were high, and we lost five tanks, but the village was captured.

Cpl Skip Ricketts 'A' Squadron

THEY ALSO SERVED

I cannot record my 'personal glimpses' without making a sincere tribute to those many other service personnel without whose efforts none of us would have survived for more than a few days, so thank you to: –

The Royal Army Service Corps, whose efforts ensured that we received supplies of food, ammunition, cigarettes, and other essentials.

The Army Postal Services, who always strove to see that the mail reached us with as little delay as possible, and helped our morale beyond description.

The Royal Army Medical Corps, who in both forward dressing stations and hospitals not far behind the lines, tended the injured and the dying.

The Royal Air Force Evacuation Service, who flew so many back to base hospitals in the UK.

The Royal Army Nursing Services and the Women's Auxiliary Nursing Service, The Queen Alexander Nursing Service, and many other volunteers, who gave what comfort they could, often under enemy fire.

The Pioneer Corps, who had the dirty work to do; clearing up the debris of war and removing and burying the dead.

The Royal Army Ordnance Corp, who recovered and repaired so many of our vehicles, and always did their best to ensure that our personal kit and private possessions found their way back to our headquarters.

The list is endless, and their combined work and dedication was vital and essential to every man who saw war from the sharp end.

Thank you, one and all.

(Roy Howard 'A' Sqdn.)

'KNOWN UNTO GOD'

In the War Cemetery at Hottot-Les-Bagues in Normandy lies a grave bearing the inscription –

A SOLDIER OF THE 1939-1945 WAR.
A CAPTAIN RECONNAISSANCE CORPS.

At the foot of the stone is inscribed – ***KNOWN UNTO GOD.***

I first came across this grave in June 1989, during my first visit to Normandy since the invasion in June 1944. I have made great efforts to try and establish some details, which might lead to a possible identification, and I have received enormous co-operation from The War Graves Commission, but without success. They have examined their records and even their exhumation orders, but there is no information as to where the body was first found or of the date on which it was placed in this cemetery. Neither is their any record as to how it was identified as being that of a Captain or as a member of the Recce Corps. I have submitted to The War Graves Commission the names of every Captain reported as killed or missing in the Official Book of Corps Operations, 'This Band of Brothers', and all the names listed on The Roll of Honour held at the Church of All Hallows in London where the Book of Remembrance is held, and in every

case, the location of each grave has been traced throughout all of the 27 countries in which the Corps operated. With some difficulty I have managed to discover that the casualty lists of World War Two are held at The Public Records Office at Kew Richmond, but these have never been published. The Records Office have now agreed to supply me with the full casualty lists for the Reconnaissance Corps, and when these come to hand I can begin a process of elimination, and with the further help of the War Graves Commission in tracing any names not already submitted, it may perhaps be possible to reach a point where it may be said – 'Believed to be the grave of Captain —— ——'. It will never be possible to establish a positive identification, but a possibility would be better than nothing.

Roy Howard

93

ALONG THE WAY

'7 ABLE' Troop had set out in Normandy at its full strength of one Officer, one Sergeant, two Corporals and eight Troopers – twelve in all. By the time we were withdrawn to Iseghem in Belgium for our first and only rest period, there were but three, of our original number left and several of the replacements who had been posted to us to keep our numbers up to strength, had also been killed or wounded on the way; in some cases within days of joining us. Of our original twelve, we had lost my Radio/Gunner – Trooper Palmer early on, then our Troop Sergeant, Sgt Abbey and his driver Trooper Wright. Our reserve Sergeant, Joe Dunnington, Corporal Washburn and Trooper Mathews had all been killed or wounded at the same time. These were followed by the losses of two of my own drivers, Troopers Morris and Bedlow. Our original numbers had been reduced to four – a percentage of over 66% killed or wounded. Of their replacements we had also lost another three. During the Ardennes offensive which curtailed our short rest, we lost another one, our Troop Officer Lieutenant Bishop, so at the time of our final disbandment, in February 1945, of the twelve who had started, there remained only three of our number to tell the story of '7 ABLE'. I've done my best to do this, and wherever possible to get the correct dates from official sources held by the Commonwealth War Graves Commission and the Public Records Office. There may well be some discrepancies but not many.

As new men joined us straight from the Recce Training Centre to replace our casualties, the old established sense of intimacy between crews gradually diminished, and the sense of being a 'Band of Brothers' was replaced by a feeling of insecurity and our relationships became rather more distant and remote.

The newcomers did their best and the older hands tried not to show any resentment, but when long established relationships are cut short and friends are replaced by strangers things can never be quite the same in many ways. It was inevitable that survivors and newcomers became much more aware of the uncertainty of their own survival and that both today or tomorrow they themselves could be replaced.

Although they died some weeks apart by a strange coincidence the graves of Sgt Abbey and Sgt Dunnington actually lie side by side in the same cemetery at Hottot-Les-Bagues in Normandy – together with several other of our number.

The names of some of those who joined us along the way escape me, but I can still picture their faces as clearly as though it had been only yesterday.

Rest in peace, you are not forgotten.

Roy Howard

HOTTOT-LES-BAGUES
WAR CEMETERY – NORMANDY

1. Sgt. Bill Abbey 5248541, 23rd June 1944, Age 34, Grave Ref. III.F.7.
2. Sgt. Joe Dunnington 4800261, 5th August 1944, Age 29, Grave Ref. IX. D. 7.

Sgt. Bill Abbey had been killed in an earlier patrol and had been replaced by Sgt. Joe Dunnington. A 'booby-trap' bomb later killed Sgt. Dunnington; Cpl. Roy Howard then became Troop Sgt.

Later photographs show Roy Howard wearing Sergeant stripes, but his war record states his rank as 'War Substantive Corporal'.

1. *Tpr. Joe Collier 10602535, 15th June 1944, Age 22, Grave Ref. III. F. 5.*
2. *Sgt. Griffiths 5114831, 15th June 1944, Age 26, Grave Ref. III. F. 6.*
3. *Tpr. John Webb 14277079, 15th June 1944, Age 26, Grave Ref. IX. E. 10.*
4. *Tpr. McHugh 10602576, 15th June 1944, Age 22, Grave Ref. II. A.1.*
    Joe Collier, Bill Griffiths, Jack Webb and Jock McHugh died on Thursday morning the week after D-Day when their Bren gun carrier ran over a massive mine.

HOTTON WAR CEMETERY –
LUXEMBOURG BELGIUM ARDENNES

1. *Tpr. Steward 4544055, 4th January 1945, Age 29, Grave Ref. V. B. 9.*
2. *Sgt. Edwards 5384009, 4th January 1945, Age 25, Grave Ref. V. B. 10.*
3. *Cpl. Metcalfe 10602579, 4th January 1945, Age 22, Grave Ref. VIII. E. 12.*
4. *Sgt. Young 3056568, 4th January 1945, Age 25, Grave Ref. VIII. E. 11.*
5. *(left) Tpr.Collingwood 5187667, 30th December 1944, Age 27, Grave Ref. VII.B.6.**
   (right) Tpr.Carter 14646512, 30th December 1944, Age 20, Grave Ref. VII.B.7.*

   * Whilst laying a tribute at these graves in 1990, Roy was particularly distressed, and later explained the tragic circumstances surrounding their deaths. Apparently they were advancing towards the front, when their vehicle was forced off the road by an American lorry driving at speed straight towards them, in full flight from the advancing Germans. Their armoured car overturned and rolled down an embankment bursting into flames. Roy described how he administered morphine to relieve the suffering of one man as he lay dying trapped inside. – The American lorry didn't stop, and was probably unaware of the tragedy they had caused.

53RD RECCE (HOLLAND)

1. *Eersel – Holland 1944.*
2. *53rd Recce Eersel Holland.*
3. *Oosterbeek – Holland (Photos – Imperial War Museum)*

61ST RECCE (FRANCE)

1. The 61st Reconnaissance Regiment: - FALAISE (Photo – Imperial War Museum)
2. 61st Recce Humber Armoured Car: - BOUVAIS (Photo – Imperial War Museum)

7 ABLE TROOP – (A SQUADRON)

1. *7 Troop on a Humber Heavy Mk. IV.*
2. *Trooper Fred Nicholls 7 A Troop A Sqdn.*
3. *ISEGHEM BELGIUM 1945. Top: Frank Palmer, Ron Burford. Middle: Fred Nickolls, Fred Pedley, -----? George Harris, Ernie Brobbin. Bottom: Sgt. Roy Howard, Lt. -----?, Ian McEnzie.*

RECONNAISSANCE IN DEPTH – OR HOWARD'S (HOLLAND) WAY

(Newsletter Old Comrades Association)

The object of this 'Spartan Exercise' could have been to attack the Dutch Bulb Fields – which as he failed to do so, this story could well be described as a reconnaissance in depth, but a complete failure to reach target. So 04.00 hrs one morning in May '86, Edna and Roy, as guests of Edna's sister and her husband, duly moved off from Shrewsbury for the Harwich – Hook line. Down Memory Ways through memory lanes of Beds and Herts, crossing Eastwards passing spider huts of Colchester to make good time at Harwich – only to suffer like days of yore with a four-hour hangabout while DM 11s sort out LST gear-box problems. Anyway, smooth crossing to arrive Hook of Holland at midnight and roll on to beaches for a three hour drive (after finding out the hard way which side of the road they use) to harbour in forest camp of Volkenswaard, Province of Brabant. Haversack rations, vehicle maintenance (echoes of 'I want them tyres cleaned of seawater') and maps marked up for Eindhoven, which surprisingly reached, and nostalgia taking over as move forward to Son – interesting canal bridge rises vertically to allow passing of boats beneath. On to St Oedenrode, very nice place and ideal for brew up. Push on to Veghel – Uden – Zeeland – Grave (recollection of shells dropping when last on bridge) – Nijmegen (of many memories) and across to 'Island'.

Oosterhout – Elst – Zetten – Driel (you're not looking at your map, Coughtrey) – Island now much more built up and many factories too. Recce on foot, still aware of anti personnel mines etc, and mused at the number of good meals at expense of a shot pig, suitably bled and cooked by Ernie Brobbin and other members of 7A Troop. Crossed Rhine via new bridge and followed riverbank along to famous Arnhem Bridge. Parking beside the Rhine (and resisting urge to take a leak) climbed steep steps (not good for C3 med cats) up to road level where we stood (at full risk of lunatic drivers, rally of Citroen cars speeding on 'Paris – Moscow – Paris' run) to read with some reverence the Plaque erected to the Memory of the Allied Airborne Troops and their great and gallant endeavour.

Returned via Heesh – S'Hertogenbosh – Oisterwijk – Hoogeloon….. paused here to visit old friends of hosts, and were given photos taken in 1944 of Recce Armoured Car – believed to have been 53rd (W) Welsh Recce who liberated that village. Visited friends at Eersel after night's harbour at De Kempervennen, and visited by son of family to take ride on back of his 1100cc Yamaha M/C. (No doubt wishing to put the wind up an old soldier like Roy) Fool that I am, I accepted with delight, and hanging on for dear life was sped through forest trails and tracks and across the border into Belgium, then via Dessel – Mol – Balen – Gheel – Leopoldburg, taking note as best he could of the Albert Canal. Most stimulating ride physically and mentally, says Roy, but did very little for my Arteriosclerosis or my Ischaemic Heart Disease (good job you printed that lot Roy or I would have been in it! – Ed.) You can only die once so they say! Finally returned to Hook of Holland via Eindhoven – Tilburg – Breda – Dordrecht – and Rotterdam to embark LST Keningin Beatrix, newly launched '86, arriving Harwich 22.00 hrs 10th May: 1000 mile wonderful trip with near perfect weather and in spite of radiation count from Russian power station accident. (Bet your bones show green in the dark.) The travels coinciding with VE Day, was surprised and pleased to note the number of flags flown from private houses on 5th May in celebration thereof.....

Thank you Roy for the interesting report which will surely bring back memories to the many who covered the journey 42 years ago....and Roy and Edna delighted to receive phone call from Den Dolby from Adelaide. Down-Under – reports well and FFI and sends greetings to all 61st.....

WAS IT ALL WORTH WHILE?

What has been written here is not a history of war, nor an academic exercise in story writing. It is more an opening of floodgates to release memories and impressions of what things were like so many years ago. Like Pandora's box, once the lid has been removed, memories escape, memories which had long been put away and laid to one side. Something of those days has now been revealed and all I can say is that I am glad that I was there to share such times with so many good comrades.

I was spared, and if those who were not were to ask me now – 'was it worth while?' – I couldn't answer them. At the time I would have said yes, but now I don't know. They do not know what tomorrow brought because they had no tomorrow. The world goes on, and the big armament firms make even bigger profits and bigger weapons – and use them! Politicians still spout out their rhetoric as loud as they ever did, but as you know, old comrades, neither armament makers nor politicians share your overcrowded cemeteries across the world. Since your day, there has been Korea, Vietnam, Cambodia, Iran, Iraq, the Falklands, Northern Ireland and many other conflicts. Little has changed in the ways of those in power. It probably never will, so – was it all worth while? I hate to tell you that it wasn't! War still holds its fascination and magic, and the young men of today still respond as you did in the past, and pay the price.....

Roy Howard

From little towns in a far land we come,
To save our honour and a world aflame.
By little towns in a far land we sleep;
And trust that world we won for you to keep!

(Rudyard Kipling)

POET'S CORNER

FOR THE FALLEN

They went with songs to the battle, they were young,
Straight of limb, true of eye, steady and aglow,
They were staunch to the end against odds uncounted,
They fell with faces to the foe.

They shall not grow old, as we that are left grow old:
Age shall not weary them nor the years condemn,
At the going down of the sun and in the morning,
We will remember them.

They mingle not with their laughing comrades again,
They sit no more at familiar tables of home:
They have no lot in our labour of the daytime:
They sleep beyond England's foam ....

Laurence Binyon
(1869-1943)

A MILITARY OBSERVER BLOWS 61 RECCE TRUMPET

(Newsletter Old Comrades Association)

Percy Barker kindly forwarded the following Report written by a Military Observer as recorded in "MILITARY AFFAIRS No. 28" dated 22nd January 1945.

"THE 61ST RECCE REGIMENT"

" The Recce Regiment which went ahead of our main striking force in the Ardennes Battle was the 61st Recce Regiment.

Formerly the Recce Regiment of a famous British Division, the 61st have seen almost continuous action since D. Day, and were the first to break out of the bridgehead on D Plus 2. It was the only Recce Regiment to be employed in the breakthrough into Holland.

Men of this Regiment were the first to enter Lille, Oudenarde and Ghent. On one occasion their leading vehicles were 65 miles ahead of their infantry, and all were actively engaged. They took part in the Escault Battle, and to date have taken 4,000 German Prisoners, their best day's bag numbering 1,000.

In the German Christmas offensive the Regiment was switched to the Ardennes, and the men, although working in completely unknown country miles ahead of our main forces, sent back such valuable information of the disposition of enemy troops that our advance went ahead smoothly."

Thank you Percy. Many will not have seen the film "Battle of the Bulge" – having already seen the play!   Ed. TT 41

VETERAN DEMOBBED.

Recently demobbed was one of the Army's longest serving veterans after seeing action all over the world.
It was a mobile field bakery nicknamed Lizzie.
She was reckoned to be at least 60 years old and had served in North Africa and Italy during the 1939 – 1945 War. More recently the van had been to the Falklands.

LIBERATED BELSEN WOMAN APPEAL.

George Rowson, 43rd Recce, has responded to a plea among the troops who freed her from Belsen when liberated on 16th April 1945. George was one of a group of nine allied soldiers first in Belsen and thinks the man Mrs. K is looking for was alongside him. Mrs. K described her saviour as probably Jewish because he had been able to rescue his own wife and sister from Belsen, taken there by the Nazis from an occupied British Colony.

Ed. TT 41

MY BIT: FROM RICHMOND, YORKSHIRE, TO EUROPE

By Don Aiken - (BBC Peoples War History web site)

1943 (Spring):

Just turned 18. Called up for the Army. Reported to Richmond Barracks (Yorkshire)

Began Primary Training in Catterick Training Camp; near Richmond.

After 6 weeks Preliminary training, posted to the Reconnaissance Training Unit in Scarborough. We were housed in several totally empty (bare boards - no furniture) hotels near the sea front, and trained by a motley selection of instructors (Officers & NCOs) from a multitude of different Infantry regiments.

Each one trying to prove that his Regiment was the best by being the biggest b . . . . . . of them all. There were so many 'Quarters' to guard and so many extra duties to do, because of the splintered nature of the unit, that life was almost an endless roundabout of training, guard duties and fatigues. As if that wasn't enough of a test, for green young lads, the physical training was extremely arduous. It typically would consist of, on reveille, a 6 mile run or else a charge into the sea. In the afternoon there would be a 2 hour session of Physical Training (usually culminating in another cross country run). As I was never any good at long distance running, and as the final few to return from a run were charged with 'malingering', and as the automatic sentence was extra physical training, it became something of a nightmare. Indeed what seemed to be the last straw was imposed on us at varying intervals, a real nightmare - Night route marches! Starting around 11 p.m. we would be marched off, in full 'field service marching order' to 10 mile route marches. These had the effect, largely due to the unyielding nature of new army boots, of creating huge blisters on large areas of both my feet and I was compelled to report to the Medical Officer for treatment. The M.O. was an 'old sweat' of a Major who sported a curly black moustache. I was marched in front of him and he asked what was wrong with me. His response to my complaint was - " You know what's the best treatment for blisters lad? Bloody well walk on 'em!" So that's what I did.

Thankfully, after a few weeks of this, we were sent on home leave; which gave me chance to recover, under the concerned ministrations of my Mum; and shortly afterwards the unit was broken up and we were sent to a new Reconnaissance Training Centre which consisted of an amalgamation of the other ex training unit from Scotland and ourselves.

This was situated in a large Camp in Catterick, near to where I had done my Primary training. Catterick had the reputation of being sheer Hell, as you might expect. But after our experiences in Scarborough I found it to be comparatively cushy. Apart from the occasional guard duty, the odd fatigue, and the unavoidable occasional 'Jankers', there was much more opportunity to enjoy the camaraderie of army life.

The training here was much more inclined to teaching, rather than physical punishment and, although general training as an all-round soldier still continued, my training as a 'Driver / Radio Operator' reached it's successful conclusion.

1943 (Winter):

From Catterick I was posted to the 61st.Reconnaissance Regt. who were encamped in Nissen huts near Cambridge. They had been doing duty in Northern Ireland for the previous part of the war, but had now been split from their Division (the 61st. Infantry Div.) to become the Reconnaissance Regt. for the 50th. Infantry Division.

The 50th. (Northumberland) Division was recently returned from North Africa and were renowned as 'The Desert Rats'. The sign (or flash) which was worn on the side of the shoulder was TT , which represented Tyne and Tees.

As my new regiment had been left undisturbed for a very unusual length of time, the troops had become very accustomed to each other and had grown into a close, even clannish, relationship. This made it very difficult for newcomers to be an accepted part of their lives, especially if the interloper was a young 'new recruit'.

Although I was accepted quite readily as a member of the Troop to which I was assigned, and was never given any sort of hard time, it seemed a long time before I too became part of the clan.

We didn't stay in any location for very long. Just a few weeks at a time before we moved on from one Nissen hutted camp to another. Norfolk was next, then on to Folkstone in Kent.

1944 (Spring):

Finally we moved to a tented camp close to a small village named Romsey, about 10 miles from Southampton.

It soon became obvious that everything was being assembled and prepared for the invasion of Europe; the long awaited Second Front.

All around us were similar camps containing troops of all persuasions. British, American, Canadian and smaller units of many other nations were all crowded into encampments that seemed to be everywhere in the fields and woods around the borders of the New Forest.

A news blackout was enforced on everyone and all leave was stopped. All mail was strictly censored.

I had received news from my brother Arthur that he had been stationed just on the outskirts of Southampton - his section of the Corps of Signals was engaged in running telephone lines between all the multitude of units which were moving in. We both managed to get a few hours of compassionate leave, and we met in Southampton one afternoon. He took me back up to his section quarters where we had a cup of tea and a chat before we bade each other farewell.

After a few weeks of the total monotony of being incarcerated in the frugal surroundings of a tented camp, which had only briefly been relieved by separate 'pep-talk' visits by the King and Field Marshal Montgomery, and by the occasional false alarm; it was good news to be told that "This is it!"

June 5th. 1944:

We packed up our gear and loaded up the armoured cars, and other means of transport, and rolled out of the camp. We snaked along down country roads, which were lined, on either side by other army vehicles waiting for their turn to move out.

Eventually we arrived in Southampton and I was surprised to see how many of the local people seemed to realise that this was for real, which was evidenced by the unusually warm waves we were given. The embarkation organisation was wonderfully efficient, and it didn't take very long for us to be installed on a U.S.A. Landing Ship Tank (LST).

The assault units of the invasion Army were in fact only at half their normal strength - the troops that were to land on 'D' Day were now being loaded, and the 'build-up' of the remainder would take place as soon as possible after the invasion. It was anticipated to be completed about 6 days afterwards. - In fact it took about 16 days because of the inclement weather that followed 'D' Day.

The entire docking facility as far as the eye could see was jam-packed with shipping of all shapes and sizes, and as most of them sported their own anti-aircraft barrage balloon, I foolishly felt a kind of festive air about it all. We bedded down wherever we could find a convenient spot, our Troop elected for the open deck (we had been issued on board with a personal burial bag which helped to keep us warm), and our ship slipped out of harbour to make way for more boats to load up. We threaded our way past the Needles rocks, which skirt the western side of the Isle of Wight and headed out into the English Channel.

The LST, which we had been assigned, had, we were told, been on several previous landings at various stages of its history; and as a consequence the bottom of the ship was deemed to be too thin to attempt another crash landing. The plan was to drop anchor about half a mile from the shore and then transfer the vehicles onto flat decked ferry type rafts, called Rhinos, which would deliver us into the shallow waters.

Two of these Rhinos were being taken over with us, one being towed astern and the other being lashed alongside. The one being towed was manned by two Army Engineers. The one alongside seemed to be intent on crashing it's way through the side of the ship as we rolled about in the choppy seas.

'D' Day - 6th. June 1944:

When dawn broke we were met by the unforgettable sight of hundreds of ships spread out as far as the eye could see. All plodding on in the same direction, towards the Normandy coast. All of them, except for the few large supply ships, were pitching and rolling to an alarming degree. Many of our men were somewhat sea-sick but luckily I have a strong stomach for such things and wasn't troubled by it.

Halfway across the channel we were astonished to see the towed Rhino suddenly become untowed! The line with which it had been attached had somehow parted, and away it went. Our ship never slackened its pace and we watched as the Rhino disappeared into the distance. I don't know what its fate was - or whether it's crew were pleased or sorry.

We arrived off the shore of Normandy in the late morning. 'Gold' Beach near the village of Arromanches, which was our first destination, had already been captured by the assault troops of the Hampshire Regiment, and it was now possible for vehicles to be disembarked on to the beach and directed to designated areas for the purpose of de-waterproofing the vehicles and preparing to advance into the bridgehead.

The LST dropped anchor and the remaining Rhino was untied from the side of the ship and made it's way round the bows, ready to be attached to the gangway which projected forwards when the bow doors opened.

It was then discovered that the coupling gear had been smashed and this sparked off a frenzied burst of activity to try to tie the units together with ropes. However, ropes are flexible by necessity, and the choppy seas made it almost impossible to hold both units in line; but with the aid of a couple of small motor-boats, pushing away like tug boats, they became near enough to go for it and our Troop made the transfer across. Soon we were running in to the beach and the Rhino bottomed out. The light armoured car (Recce Car) in which I was a crew member was the first to drive off, and in my elevated position in the turret I felt like a submarine commander, especially when we suddenly dropped into a bomb hole which was concealed beneath the water and only the turret was left exposed.

The Beach Party had been well trained for this situation and had the de-waterproofing area completely organised and running smoothly. Although I almost threw a spanner in the works!

My armoured car had been fitted with a device, which I had contrived, to allow me to operate the smoke canister gun without having to lean outside the turret. Basically, it was a bike brake mechanism, which was attached at one end to the gun, and, at the other end, the brake grip was attached to my seat support.

Whilst the driver was removing the waterproofing from the engine, the Officer went to a quick '0' Group (Officers briefing) and the radio-operators tuned in their radio transmitters to the H.Q. transmitter. This was quite a delicate operation and it was at its finest point when my elbow touched against the trigger. Bang! went the smoke discharger - and as I quickly bobbed my head out I could see the smoke bomb heading straight into the middle of a wired off field, with dozens of painted notices showing the sign of a skull and cross-bones and the words "Achtung Minen". Which didn't take a genius to recognise that my bomb was landing in a German mine-field, and the mines were too close for comfort.

I ducked down inside my turret and held my breath........

Nothing - oh good! Then Bang! Bang! Bang! ..... I realised it was someone banging on the turret. When I popped my head back out I was confronted with the angry face of the Beach Officer - a Major - whose features reminded me strongly of the Medical Officer with whom I had been acquainted in Scarborough; complete with black curly moustache, but perhaps even stronger on the language!

Soon the various sections of our Regiment were ready to move off to try to reach their pre-arranged target locations. Ours was a wooded hill about 15 miles inland, and our role was to 'seize and hold' it, until the main body of troops could relieve us. It was soon quite obvious that, because of our delayed landing, there was no possibility of us reaching our target that day.

Nevertheless, we 'bashed on regardless' and made our way down the sunken country lanes, which are typical of Normandy. Eventually we were given the order to 'harbour' down for the night and we drove into a tree-lined field, concealing the vehicles around the perimeter.

It seemed that no one had any idea what our position was, and what the situation was around us. We got news that our Colonel, a typical Cavalry Officer, had been riding in a Bren-carrier (a small tracked vehicle with no turret). He had been standing up, in a 'tally-ho!' type of manner, when a German sniper, who was concealed in the ditch alongside the road, shot him up the bum. We never saw or heard of him again.

We laid out the large waterproof cover from a Bren-carrier and a couple of Troops bedded down underneath it. I assume that every-one else did the same. Sentries were posted at various intervals, armed with Bren machine guns. A foot patrol consisting of a Sergeant (a Scotsman), a Corporal and 5 men was sent out to reconnoiter the surrounding area.

We were jolted awake in the pitch black of the night by the sharp rattle of a nearby Bren gun and loud, frantic shouting. Everyone grabbed their weapons and made for the commotion. What had occurred was this:

Whilst we were on board the LST we had been given a Password with which to challenge anyone in the expected confusion of the situation. The Password was 'Handle' and the Response was 'With Care'.

This seemed quite sensible although we had never used such a method before. The sentry who had been posted near to us was a Yorkshireman from Leeds, and not too gifted in the I.Q. factor. He had been sat behind his gun, on his own, in the dead blackness, scared stiff (as we would all have been) when he heard the stealthy scuffling noise of someone creeping up. Panic must have set in, because he shouted out the normal challenge of 'Who goes there! ' This threw the approaching Glaswegian Sergeant of our recce patrol (now returning to us) right off his stride. He responded the best way he could - "Onnle wi' kearr! Onnle wi' kearr "! he shouted. The guttural accent uttering this strange sounding cry must have sounded like Adolf Hitler himself to the panic stricken sentry, so his fingers jerked at the trigger - killing the Sergeant and wounding the Corporal in the foot,

The following days were almost as chaotic as we tried to tie everything up together. We seemed to be tearing around the countryside without much particular purpose; although I suppose it all had some plan behind it. We were making forward patrols along country roads, which were lined with trees, hedges, ditches, or raised banks; all of which were ideal cover for the enemy guns. Every now and again we would make some contact with the enemy and a skirmish would ensue. Then there would be a push forward, with our troops moving through the cornfields amongst which I remember the sight of dozens of our Self-propelled 25 pounder guns blazing away to soften up an unseen enemy.

Then one day as we moved cautiously along a narrow country road, sensing danger, we ran into an ambush of machine-guns hidden behind the hedgerow. After a short exchange of fire the Corporal who commanded my armoured car was badly wounded, his stomach having been ripped open by a stream of machine gun bullets. We decided to pull back out of the situation, and covering fire was given to carry my Corporal back to base on the front of a Bren carrier.

As my armoured car now had no commander, I was sent back to Squadron H.Q. and given the job of 'shotgun' on the 3-ton truck, which was used to bring ammunition from the dump near the invasion beach.

We set off on our first journey. The truck was driven by a Trooper and the passenger seat was occupied by a Corporal.

I was sat in the back of the soft-topped lorry; armed with a rifle.

We picked up our full load of ammunition without problem, the other members of the crew being obviously used to the procedure, and we set off to return to our H.Q. Now I was sat on 3 tons of ammunition.

It wasn't long however before I realised that our Corporal had lost his way, as we did a couple of reverses in cul de sacs etc.. Then the surroundings began to change from rural roads to rubbled streets, and we did the sharpest reverse of all when we found ourselves in the middle of a street fighting scene, which was no place for a lorry-load of ammo. We had arrived in the besieged town of Caen - a long way off our course.

Eventually we recovered our direction and as we bowled along through a little village I suddenly heard a loud bang and our truck came to a sudden halt. A detachment of infantry was positioned in the village, and there were loud shouts and frantic gesticulations in my direction. I hesitated, not knowing what could be wrong. I didn't hesitate for a second longer however when my Corporal appeared, running rapidly past me and wildly waving for me to follow.

After we had sorted ourselves out, and the Corporal had told me what he knew, we went back to our truck to arrange the next move.

What had happened was this: A lone German Messerschmitt fighter plane had spotted us making our way down the road, had turned round facing towards us and fired off a single cannon or rocket. This had hit the truck immediately in front of the driver and had blown a hole in his middle, killing him instantly. The ammunition, with me atop, had been separated from the driver by a thin wooden partition.

I was then returned to my Squadron, as a new Corporal had been found to command my armoured car. He was a Welshman named Evans, a reticent type, who never became very friendly or communicative.

The next few days continued to be quite eventful, although I have forgotten most of the detail and the sequential order of events.

Some of the village names still spring to mind; although they lack any substance. - Tilly, Hottot, Caumont, Grainville.

We continued to probe along the byways making contact with the enemy and reporting to base. One morning when my car had been leading the patrol along a particularly nasty stretch of road for a long stretch of time, it was decided to pass the job over to a Bren-Carrier Troop. We pulled in to the side of the road to let them pass through us. The leading Carrier had gone less than a hundred yards when it blew up on a land-mine, killing all the crew.

The forward movement of the invading troops all along the front gradually ground to a halt as German resistance increased and the planned occupation of Caen was thwarted again and again. The front line became almost static as both sides dug in to take up defensive positions.

Our Regiment was detailed to defend a very long, narrow wood, named Le Bois de Briquessard. We took over at night-time from an American Regiment and took up positions in fox-holes and ditches on the leading edge of the wood, facing across a field to a hedgerow, which was occupied by the enemy. Our Assault Troop sent out foot patrols at night, but there were very few incidents arising from them. The main problem was that we were a good target for the German NebelWerfers (this multi-barrelled launcher fired mortars whose bombs made a horrible wailing, or howling sound as they made their way through the air before exploding with a loud crunch somewhere in the wood). Our Regimental Field H.Q. had been set up in the middle of the wood. This received a direct hit one night and quite a large number of casualties ensued.

July 1944:
After several days in this position we were relieved by an Infantry Regt.

Apparently Lieut.General Horrocks, the Commander of XXX Corps, had noticed that we had been placed in this defensive position and ordered that we be withdrawn. He was a very experienced General, who knew how important it was to prevent his future spear-head troops from developing a defensive attitude to the war.

We were then used on small Reconnaissance foot patrols; and during one of these night patrols we were sent to try to make contact with the Germans who were thought to have infiltrated into the grounds of the nearby churchyard. The night turned out to be extremely misty and crawling through the gravestones was, in itself, a creepy business. The thought that, at any moment, a German machine gun could rattle away into your face was even more disturbing. However, we completed our search of the area without contacting any Germans, although we found a dugout, which they had recently vacated. You could always tell where Germans had been by the smell; it wasn't a repulsive smell, just strongly different - probably due to the food that they ate; German sausage perhaps.

Then we pulled back to take up defensive positions. Along with another young Trooper, I was positioned in an old German slit-trench in a hedgerow alongside a path, armed with a Bren machine-gun. We alternately manned the gun and rested.

During my rest period I was suddenly 'brought up sharp' by a burst of fire from my companion's gun. When I asked him what was wrong, he said that he had seen something move across the path. I looked for a long time (trying to suppress my fear) and then realised that the 'something' was a twig on the hedge, a few inches away, which had been disturbed by a sudden breeze in this otherwise still, dark and misty night.

There then began a gradual crumbling in the German defences as more and more pressure was exerted. We began probing again and one day as we approached the small town of Villers Bocage, on a broad front, we drew to a halt as we approached an obvious ambush point between the hedge-rows. This was a sharp bend in the road, which was dominated by a farmhouse facing straight up the road. At this moment the Assault Troop, which had been making it's way through the fields and hedgerows on our right, came under fire from German infantry and sustained some casualties.

My car was leading the patrol on the road, and every nerve was tensed for any eventuality. I was astounded when a small wicket gate, in a garden wall at the side of the house, suddenly opened and six big German S.S. troops emerged and ran across the front of the house. It was exactly like a shooting gallery at the Fairground with the ducks bobbing along from one side to the other. However, I didn't get a prize off the top shelf because I couldn't turn my turret fast enough, and my bullets merely splattered the brickwork behind them before they disappeared round the corner.

August 1944:

Then the beginnings of the break-out began, and we moved forward to take up our position. We moved into an apple orchard close to a cross-roads, which was under shell-fire. The Troop H.Q. armoured car had positioned itself in the corner of the orchard and they had dug a trench underneath it, filling in the gap below the car with a sheet of corrugated iron that they had found. The driver, down in the slit trench, had then begun to brew up tea for the troop.

We were given the signal that it was ready and I climbed out and crossed over towards the H.Q. car, along with a lad from another car, when suddenly a German shell fell short of it's target and made a direct hit on the corrugated iron sheet. The blast blew us both underneath another car and we lay there with hearts in our mouths. Then I said. I'm going to dash for it, and as I stood up and took a couple of steps I heard another shell whistling it's way towards us. The next thing that I remember is being reseated in the turret of my car.

A member of another crew, who had been watching through his periscope, swore that I had leapt from the ground, straight into the top of the turret (a height of almost 6 ft.) without touching the sides!

The tragedy was that Henry Ansell, a popular young man, had caught the full blast of the explosion, which had blown the corrugated iron into large pieces, which had torn him apart.

We advanced from there to Mt. Picon - not a mountain, but a high rising area of land with a Spot Height of 365. Here I remember seeing a Military Policeman stood on a road junction steadfastly directing the advancing convoys of Army vehicles, enveloped in clouds of red dust, and under constant bombardment from enemy shells. It was here too that we were paused for a few hours, and on investigating the familiar smell of death nearby, we found a German soldier lying in a covered slit trench. His face was a huge ball of maggots. We managed to get hold of some chloride of lime and scattered this all over him. I still remember the disgusting sight of the maggots flowing from his face like a living stream.

The American Army had now fully broken out of their less defended sector of the front, almost all the German tank forces having been thrown against the pivot point of Caen. This allowed them to partly encircle the German army from the South and a simultaneous pincer movement by our troops from the North entrapped thousands of enemy troops who were trying to flee through the only gap left at a village called Falaise.

This now became a killing field, with all the Allied gun-fire and the concentrated attacks by our rocket-firing dive-bombers (Typhoons) being rained down on the fleeing Germans. Thousands of the enemy were killed and, as we passed through the devastated area in pursuit of those who had managed to escape, I remember seeing bodies piled on top of bodies to a height of several feet.

The Free French Armoured Division was ordered to advance on Paris, and we moved on to the Seine, in the vicinity of Vernon, and there we indulged in the luxury of a short bathe in the river.

Now the advance was in full flow. Our Regiment was put in as the spear-head of the advance which we did at rate of 60 miles in one day, and passing through towns whose names had been made familiar to me from stories of the First World War, which took place here thirty years earlier, Amiens, the Somme, Cambrai, Arras, Lille and Armentieres. Places which had been fought over for months, even years. We passed them by in a few days.

We were the first troops to cross the border into Belgium and at that point we were relieved by the Guards Armoured Division who passed through us and took up the spear-head.

We were then used to protect the Northern flank of the narrow corridor, which was being made through Belgium, and to prevent the escape of the remnants of the 9th. German Army which had been cut off between the corridor and the Northern coast.

We were positioned thinly along all the bridges, which crossed the Escaut Canal. At each bridge was positioned, typically, one Anti-tank gun, a section of Assault troops and one Armoured car. Although the actual coverage probably differed from bridge to bridge.

As night fell we heard the noise of gun-fire at the next bridge further down the canal, and stood ready for action when the fire had abated. It wasn't very long before we heard the noise of approaching German tanks and other vehicles. The first vehicles moved towards the bridge and we opened fire with all we had. The vehicles withdrew away from the canal and we didn't hear from them again.

We later learned that the gun-fire that we had heard from the next bridge had a little story-line to it.

It is the practice of Anti-tank gun-crews to remove part of the firing mechanism of their gun and conceal it, when they are not on stand-to, so that in the eventuality of being infiltrated by surprise, the enemy would be unable to use the gun.

This had been the case here, when suddenly they had been awakened by the look-out who had heard the approaching Germans. But they couldn't remember where the part had been hidden! Panic set in. They searched high and low - but without success. All the time the Germans were getting nearer. A very strong force, consisting of several tanks, armoured cars and field guns. Soon the leading tank was rumbling onto the bridge. Found it! Shaking fingers put the mechanism together; nervous hands adjusted the sights. Then, when the tank was already in the centre of the bridge, - Bang! Bulls-eye!

After a heavy exchange of fire, the Germans took some losses because of the hidden positions of the defending guns, and there was a lull in the fighting. Then a German officer appeared carrying a white flag. The Officer in charge of the bridge defenders met him on the bridge, where it was agreed for the Germans to remove their dead and wounded on condition that they moved back and didn't return. A funny episode, which couldn't have worked out better if it, had all been planned.

September 1944:

It had been decided to strike up through Holland on a narrow front in an attempt to seize a corridor which would reach over the Rhine and into Germany; opening up the way to Berlin.

Airborne Troops were dropped on a line up through Holland with the objective of capturing all the bridges on the line of advance.

XXX Corps would quickly create the corridor and take over from the airborne troops. The first line of smaller bridges was to be captured by the US Airborne; and the last one (at Arnhem) was to be taken by the British Airborne Troops.

Initially everything went quite well. The advance progressed rapidly; and it was during this time, whilst we were moving up behind the Guards Armoured Division, that Monty stopped his staff-car, had a few words with us and handed out some packets of fags. Very welcome!

In a few days XXX Corps had arrived at Nijmegen and captured the large bridge over the Waal. When we arrived at Nijmegen the battle for Arnhem, a few miles up the road, was taking place. This was doomed to failure, as history knows, and I won't add to it here.

The result was that the whole advance bogged down and, with the approaching winter, conditions would soon be unfit to make a further assault to cross the Rhine. We took up various defensive positions along the perimeter of our territory and a few minor successes were achieved up and down the line but it became obvious that we weren't going anywhere for a while. At this point it was decided to consolidate and regroup.

Part of this regrouping meant that 50th. Division, which had been badly reduced in strength, would be disbanded and broken up to make up losses in other Divisions.

December 1944:

With this in mind we, the 50th's Reconnaissance Regt., were sent back to a small town called Iseghem, which is situated in Belgium, close to the French border. We were billeted in various houses, cafés and so on, and our H.Q. and cook-house was situated in the railway goods yard. All our vehicles and equipment were taken to a dump somewhere on the road to Antwerp. We had a few days of wonderful bliss. Nothing to do but have a few drinks in the cafés and idle our time away.

We hadn't reckoned on the Germans. They had realised that the defensive strength of the US Army in the Belgian Ardennes forest was not good, with only 4 Divisions holding a front of 80 miles long.

Hitler himself had ordered 3 Armies, totalling twenty-one Divisions (although well below strength), to be assembled in Germany ready for a huge counter-attack.

This began on December 16th, meeting with great initial success and the American defence lines were cut to ribbons.

The situation was becoming very serious, as the whole 'sharp-end' of the Allied forces were in danger of being isolated.

The British forces directed a push down from the north onto the advancing Germans. We were given 24 hours to reclaim our vehicles and equipment and move out to the Ardennes. This we did.

We arrived at Namur a few days before Christmas, and were immediately given the task of contacting a forward unit of US Engineers who had been instructed to blow a bridge over a small river whenever they sighted the German advance. The orders had now been changed to 'blow up the bridge regardless', but radio contact with the Engineers had been lost.

We set off on our mission and we were shocked to see convoys of US troops retreating in total panic. They threw us some fags and shouted that we were going the wrong way.

We approached our destination, and turned a corner to see that the road ran down into a steep valley, with a similar road running round and down the cliffs on the other side. At that moment we heard a loud explosion and knew that the bridge had been blown. We continued for a short way down the road before spotting the US Engineers running up behind the hedgerow and waited for them to arrive. It was then that I observed a German tank on the road across the valley and, almost immediately, a puff of smoke from his 88 mm. gun. There was a whoosh as the shell screamed over my head and took a lump out of the road and part of the tyre from the armoured car, which stood a few yards behind me. Within a few seconds our armoured cars had disappeared up the road and round the corner, in reverse.

Christmas Day saw the peak of the German advance, and I remember that on that day on returning to base, after a bitter cold day of patrolling through the snowy forests, we were all handed a Christmas celebratory bottle of beer. When I opened my bottle and tried to drink from it - nothing came out - the beer was frozen solid! The only solution was to break the bottle and lick the beer like an iced-lolly.

We spent the next few days in patrolling the hills and woods of the Ardennes, amongst the thick snow and ice which often made the forest trees look like fairyland. In the end the German offensive failed to break through the defences and ground to a halt.

January 1945:

It was now clear that the bold gamble had failed. The German losses had been very heavy and probably ended any possibility of Germany continuing to defy defeat. His last defensive barrier was the River Rhine, and that was going to be the next target.

Meanwhile we were returned to Iseghem, in Belgium, to continue our little rest and to be notified of our new postings.

February 1945:
I had been posted to the 52nd. Reconnaissance Regt., which was the Recce for 52nd. Lowland Scottish Division. We were given the 'MOUNTAIN' shoulder flash to sew on our tunics, along with the St. Andrew's Shield. They were a Division which had been stationed in Scotland for a long time, training for mountain combat in preparation for a possible invasion of Norway. However their first slice of action came when they left England about 2 months after 'D' Day to capture some islands off the Dutch coast. There probably wasn't a mountain for a hundred miles.

I was at last able to fully take up my role as a 'Driver/Operator' rather than a 'Gunner/Operator' because the Scout-cars in this Regt. were Daimlers, not Humbers, and the light armoured cars were manned only by two men, the Commander and the Driver/Radio Operator. These were wonderful vehicles, highly manoeuvrable, and fitted with pre-select gears and the ability to change gear whilst in reverse selection; theoretically allowing the car to go as fast in reverse as forwards.

The Army pressed forward towards the Rhine with one or two spells of heavy fighting. Then, around this time, I was given some home leave.

March 1945:
After a few happy days at home, I bade a tearful farewell and returned to my Unit.

The whole force was now intent on pressing on into Germany. After some heavy fighting on all fronts (because the Germans were desperate to prevent us doing so) we, the leading troops at that time, eventually succeeded in reaching the Rhine.

The Infantry were then brought through to hold the line and we were pulled back about a mile from the river. We settled in the cellar of a cottage and awaited our next mission, which we knew wouldn't be long because of the intense and heavy build up of men and equipment in preparation for a crossing. During a lull in the gunfire one of the lads in my troop spotted a horse in a paddock alongside the cottage, and decided to ride it. He mounted the horse and had a great time trotting around. Then came a single shot (probably from a German 88 mm. anti-tank gun) which blew his head off.

We had a request for Radio Operator volunteers to be detached to the Royal Engineers on the forthcoming crossing of the Rhine for the purpose of communications. Although soldiers didn't usually believe in volunteering, I was new in this unit and wouldn't miss the company much, so I volunteered.

I was taken (along with another Operator) in a small truck, back into Belgium; where we were attached to different Companies of Engineers, placed in Heavy Armoured cars and moved back into Germany.

My car was moved up behind a huge earth banking, which ran all along both sides of the Rhine in this area, used to prevent flooding of this very low-lying and flat countryside.

The communications set-up was this: The Officer in Charge of the Royal Engineers Unit would radio his messages to an armoured car, which was situated near to mine. This message would be relayed to me by means of a runner. I would then send this back to Divisional H.Q.

Remember that these radios had a very limited range; especially the back-pack field radios used by the forward engineers.

March 23rd. 1945:
Then the attack started. In it's own way it was almost as awe inspiring as the 'D' Day landings. It was preceded by a massive airborne assault; with hundreds of gliders flying low over our heads and landing behind the enemy lines. The biggest artillery bombardment ever to be carried out followed immediately behind. Hundreds upon hundreds of heavy artillery opened up all at once, with thousands of shells whistling overhead. The noise was deafening.

Then the ground troops started to move through us and down to the river bank. The Royal Engineers began to build the pontoon bridges, which would allow the rest of the Division to cross over. This was done under very heavy German fire, as most of their first line defensive positions, dug into the huge earth banking on the German side of the river, had not been affected by the artillery or by the airborne attack behind them. I don't know what the cost was to the Engineers, but it must have been high.

I was kept fully occupied sending the coded messages back to H.Q. and occasionally receiving some back.

Then there was a sudden drop in radio activity and I found time to poke my head out of the turret, only to find that the lull in getting messages had been caused by a German shell which had landed close and killed the runner.

In a few hours we knew that the bridge had been constructed across the Rhine and that the infantry were already across and being followed by tanks. The sounds of warfare became a little more distant and we moved forward to get a good view of the proceedings. The pontoon bridge was thick with movement, as it had now become a two way highway. All the paraphernalia of an attacking army was crossing into Germany. The rattle of our infantry's small-arms fire coming from the enemy positions was now resulting in long lines of German soldiers being marched out of Germany to P.O.W. camps somewhere in England.

April 1945:
This truly was the beginning of the end for the Germans. The Rhine had been crossed at many points and the British and US Armies were pouring across Germany. When I rejoined my unit (I remember catching them up as a passenger in a Bren-carrier) we were leading the advance Northwards to the North Sea port of Bremen (Bremerhaven).

We reached the outskirts of Bremen, and the last target line on our map; and moved into a small villa situated opposite a Displaced Persons Camp. After checking the surrounding ground, we posted a look-out and settled down for the night. In the early hours of the morning we awoke to the sound of heavy artillery shells crashing all around us. It soon became clear that the shells were originating from our own British guns, and it was a great relief when the fire finally moved on.

Apparently, due to some mix-up somewhere, our last target line on the map that night was the first target line for our artillery on the following morning.

We moved on from Bremen to a Prison Camp, called Stalag 10b, which was further East on the road to Hamburg. Here we found prisoners of all nationalities, all in a terrible state.

May 4th. 1945:

It was here that we received news of the German surrender on our front, and it was an emotional experience to sit round a big bonfire and to listen to one of our Regimental pipers playing the beautiful lament 'The Battles O'er' .

May 7th. 1945:

The unconditional surrender of all German Forces was signed. The war in Europe was at last over.

May 8th. 1945:

This was officially nominated as V.E. (Victory in Europe) Day.

Because our Senior Officers considered it to be undesirable for us to be allowed to celebrate 'on the loose' amongst the German population, a decision that I could never appreciate, we were confined to our base and spent the day 'bulling-up' our vehicles with a mixture of paraffin and engine oil. A procedure which made them look great, for a day or two until the dust had stuck all over the oil.

When I later saw pictures of the great celebrations, in such places as Trafalgar Square, I was a bit displeased.

We then moved East to occupy a town named Salzwedel, which was later to become part of Eastern Germany and shut off behind the Iron Curtain.

The next few months were a series of moves around the Ruhr (the industrial centre of Germany) in the vicinity of Cologne, Dusseldorf and Munster. Much of our duties were of Police patrol type work.

Germany had used millions of foreign workers as slave-labour, in the North of Germany in particular. These had of course now been given their freedom and were becoming a huge problem. They had a deep hatred of their previous masters.

Most of them were of Eastern European origin and were either not wanted by their own countries or did not want to return. Instead they wandered around the country-side raping and looting.

We would sometimes be posted at a German Police station and respond to emergency calls out in the country-side.

When things were settling down, our Regiment moved to a small village called Freckenhorst, near Warendorf, which is in turn situated between Munster and Bielefeld. This was a much more settled existence and everything was organised much more on Army camp lines. We had very little work to do, and time was spent in playing games of various sorts, or down in the Canteen, which had been established in a big café.

A football Cup Competition was organised, and our Troop team won it. The goal-keeper on the other side was a Captain; and his face was a picture when I headed the ball out of his hands to score the winning goal.

The Colonel (Lt.Col.Stormont-Darling) was a keen Rugby player and he organised a Regimental rugby team. As we were a small unit, and as Rugby had a restricted following, I became one of the team. We weren't a very formidable side and I remember travelling to play a team from the R.A.F. at a big aerodrome in Northern Germany. We were thrashed unmercifully, and I seemed to spend more time being thrown out of touch, along with the ball, than running with it down the field.

During the following months many of the older members of the Regiment were being demobilised and returned to civilian life in England, and this was an on-going exercise with men waiting their turn in a 'first-in first-out' basis. This of course meant that the army was being rapidly reduced in size and a continual re-organisation of Units was necessary.

I can't help but marvel at the tremendous organisation, which managed to keep abreast of all the massive changes, which took place.

Units, which had been created during the war, were the first to be disbanded. The Reconnaissance Corps was typical of this origin and was disbanded. Our Regiment merged with the Lothian and Border Horse and we continued on almost as before except with a different cap-badge. A 'wheat sheaf', instead of the 'arrow supported by two lightning flashes' which had been our badge

This wasn't to last more than a month or two, as it came the turn of the Territorial Army units to be disbanded.

The Lothian and Border Horse had to go! In came the Fife and Forfar Yeomanry and for a brief few weeks we sported the Clenched Fist badge on our berets. But they were living on borrowed time and soon we were marching out of Freckenhorst to be transported to various regular army units whose function was similar to Reconnaissance.

I was to join the 14th./20th. King's Hussars - another cap-badge - The Austrian Eagle.

I arrived at the ex German Army Barracks in Wuppertal, which is in the Ruhr. The barracks was situated on the top of a hill overlooking the large town. Further along the top of the hill was another barracks occupied by the 2nd. Battalion of the Grenadier Guards.

The 14/20th had previously been in the Italian Campaign and had fought alongside the Gurkha Regt. with some distinction, and had been presented with the honour of wearing the badge of the Gurkhas on the sleeve of their tunics. This was the 'crossed Kukris' (Curved knives) and was another bit of brass to polish.

They had different equipment than I had been used to, and it made the life of 'waiting for Demob' much more interesting. I had been given the job of training and organising the Radio Operators in my Squadron. The details were left entirely to my own discretion, as many of the Officers too were 'waiting for Demob'. This meant that many happy days were spent swanning around the surrounding country-side in the exciting new tanks with which we were equipped, pretending to be on some sort of Exercise.

The town of Wuppertal was an interesting place. It was a long, narrow town, situated in a valley with a small river running along its length. Elevated above the river was an over-head railway, the 'SchweberBahn' which had elevated stations positioned all along the way. This was a wonderful transport system which worked very well, even in a town which had been bombed to rubble; which was typical of all the Ruhr towns. Then, after about another year of waiting, it was, at long last, my turn to go home - for good.

Don Aiken

'DADS BROWN DIARY'

(Kindly supplied by Derek Brewer)

TROOPER ERIC BREWER 14631319 – 61ST RECCE 13 TROOP 'B'SQDN.

(1942 diary, but used for 1944)

The following pages have been contributed by Derek Brewer, copied directly from his father's pocket diaries of the time, and transcribed exactly as they were written then.

Grateful thanks to Derek and the Brewer family for kindly allowing me to include it in this work.

Another diary starts on Wednesday, 17th May 1933 but this is likely to relate to 17th May 1944.

Here, Dad enters:

Water proofing armoured car.

He enters for the next three days, on each day:

Water Proofing.

On the 21st May, Dad writes

On waterproofing half-track.

It continues:
22nd May 1944: Got 10/- extra change from NAFI
23rd May 1944: SGTS MESS not a bad job
24th May 1944: SGTS MESS
25th May 1944: SGTS MESS
26th May 1944: SGTS MESS
27th May 1944: SGTS MESS
28th May 1944: SGTS MESS
29th May 1944: Sent shave foam and other oil (?)
30th May 1944: AT SGTS MESS
31st May 1944: In charge of Sergeants' Mess
1st June 1944: Gerry would like to know what we know
2nd June 1944: If people only knew the date of the 2nd front

3rd June 1944: Had briefing and have been told all about Second front.
4th June 1944: Boarded ship at Southampton still in dock. Had final briefing today.
5th June 1944: Still in Southampton docks on board ship. Left port 6.40 for France.

1942 Diary

June 6th: Landed in France at 7.30 at the right of "Port Embasie" the beach is filled with stuff and plenty of dead lying about, Gerry gun positions have been well blasted all the crews were killed from concussion, the shell craters are as big as houses and they are everywhere.
We pushed on to the Goumont Area and got lost from the rest, Spando opened up from the hedge about 2-ft away and killed carrier driver.
June 7th: Still not able to find rest of squadron so we tried to make contact but could not find them, soon loads of Gerry prisoners and in among them are Japs????? , they look consumptive you would think to look at them, found out today that Blake had been killed also 1 man injured in troop staying in harbour for night and hope to find squadron tomorrow.
June 8th: Moved off at 4 o clock to find squadron made contact with them near 103, took up positions and came across little activity.
June 9th: Moved to Bayeax to join up with the other squadron Gerry had put in counter attack on hill 103 so we returned back, large tank battle between us must be about 1000 tanks found out later that it was 1,500 tanks British in this battle, lots of snipers active bullets going everywhere and SSM.
June 10th: Still at 103 snipers still active 2 bullets scrayed by Smith also we were forced to move back to new position and take up that position.
June 11th: Left 103 made patrols in village came across machine gun post and wiped it out, then found dead Gerrys one had a good ring on him so Lacy went and took it off and was immediately opened up on by snipers but luckily he was missed.
June 12th: Shifted to Tilly and opened up on by Spondes Squadron still active.
June 13th: Now on G.P. near Granville Gerry's 500yds away not much activity.
June 14th: Still same place Carrin caught it, done recce on enemy held positions.
June 15th: Moved to 103 came across Gerry Bikes abandoned it and every thing on them found 1 mortar.
June 16th: Enemy put in counter attack but failed mostly Infantry attack plenty of Gerry infantry wiped out also many British wounded returning.
June 17th: Still in same position Gerry put in tank attack our S.D. knocking them out like flies saw 2 of our tanks get knocked out, Stayed in position all night only small arms fire and a few mortars but not too bad.
June 18th: Shifted on to Granville met stiff enemy opposition Arks and Carriers went in to try to find all positions but 88 opened up and we lost heavy Ark also a couple of Carriers total loss in men is 12, we were forced to withdraw as the 88 could pick us off like coconuts but later on tanks went in followed by Artillery and mortar fire which knocked out 88 also killed approximately 200 Gerrys.
June 19th: Went out on another Recce to find force in the Granville area we were advancing after finding out Gerrys forward O.P. also machine gun site when we opened upon by Mortar and

Spando while we were taking up defensive position it was decided to try and pin point the Gun on trying to we lost 5 men Sgt EKINS, KERSHAW, COLES, GRESTY, GARDENER, found out on July 7th that Gresty was wounded and taken prisoner. We were again forced to withdraw.

June 20th: Leaving Granville as Div 7 attack is going in went back to rear position to be reinforced, also some Gerry plane knocked down and have at last found a farm to obtain milk, things seem to be quiet only thing we have to worry about is Enemy infiltrating through our front line but every thing has been quiet and had a bath in the stream a change to get this dirt off of us.

June 21st: Things still quiet and wish they stayed like it our only Casualty has been Docady who was killed by a sneak raider machine gunning his lorry.

Have been talking to a Frenchman of the underground movement he showed us the Cross De Gaur which he won in the last war, most of these people round here are very quiet.

June 22nd: We have taken some prisoners today and are know in position near main x roads near Granville we located a Enemy patrol but were turned back.

What a day nothing to do except watch after this morning but have killed a couple of Gerry chickens which tasted okay, we hope to be going back tomorrow I hope so.

June 23rd: Still at Granville x roads hope to move tomorrow things rather quiet only a few mortars getting use to dodging them I know hope they stay far enough having to cause no harm this trench digging is just about getting me down think Ill be a grave digger after this war as all I seem to be doing is.

June 24th: What a army you don't know weather you are coming or going they decided that we should stay here, so we went on G.P. found this position and the Artillery put up a barrage followed by mortars then the Air Force strafed it with rockets and bombs later heard that there was about 500 Gerrys killed in a woods where the Barrage was the heaviest: That is according to the news.

June 25th: We made a patrol into no mans land to find enemy forward positions so that the East York's could put in attack came in contact with Gerry Forward O.P. also kit seems as though they must have seen us and pulled out fast East York's put in a attack and everything seems to be going well took main x roads.

June 26th: Once again we had to patrol no mans land to find position of Enemies O.P. and forward MG. Post advance about 2 mile came in contact with Late Green Howards position and found their kit intact which looked as though they had to get out in a hurry, while near Gerrys forward O.P. must have seen us because a couple of Mortars landed about 20 – 30 yds away so we went back.

June 27th: Found out today that the Green Howards position, which we found yesterday, are missing somewhere. A Company of 57 men altogether have not been heard of for over a week they think Gerry surrounded them and took them prisoners.

Went out on patrol to find out how effective our mortar firing was but unable to get close enough to find out because of M.G.

June 28th: Went out to hold forward position mainly a forward O.P. in case Gerrys put in a attack while the 59th are retiring us but was only in danger of our own chaps shooting on us as they did not know there was anyone in front of them these tin hats want some telling from a distance if they are Gerrys or us, but I got relived at last. I don't know first in last out as usual.

29 June: Back at Base.

Taking it easy found out casualties today are according to the O.C. are 25 killed 12 injured about another 12 Bomb happy people I know are as follows-

SGT WALLACE

SGT WHITHOUSE

About 5 SETS altogether 7 Corporals and the rest troopers about a 1/8th of squadron killed ANOTHER 1/8th injured. ? squadron killed and injured Dir Comade said that our casualties had to be less as we wad be raid for B-Pack ????

June 30th: Still at Base paid today for first time note lap pay 2007 = £1m English money.

Went to local farms and obtained 1lb butter and about 1 gallon of milk had a couple of chicken from bombed house not so bad.

Gun fire tonight is heavy weather not to bad, bags of aircraft flying about place called Therobrot.

July 1st: Moved to South of Granville to forward O.P. to Direct mortar fire. Gerry about 500 yards in front. Code/signs for mortars light or heavy shelling light or heavy also strength or movement if any. Only one mortar and two shellings all day rather quiet. Stayed there all night rather quiet only a few buckshe mortars coming over.

July 2nd: Still same place doing same job had a few enemy mortars come over but don't think he will trouble us any more by the weight of the barrage laid down. Located enemy vehicles moving. Soon had artillery firing at it.

1933 Diary entries as there are no entries in the 1942 diary

3rd July 1944: Position inspected by General and found to be possible for Gerry to come through valley.

4th July 1944: Gerry mortared to left of us but was unlucky in finding us.

5th July 1944: Back at base on 2nd, stayed in observation position all night and day.

6th July 1944: Still at base and have handed in bikes - have got ½ tracks now.

7th July 1944: Blimey! More like a holiday in ½ track. No sweating on bikes.

8th July 1944: Went to Bayeux for baths. Had look round. Still at base.

9th July 1944: Moved to Granville. Infantry took it and we have a forward position.

10th July 1944: Still at Granville and have taken up position in front of slot trenches.

11th July 1944: Mortared = cow killed and hope to have steak for tea, everyone okay except 2 injured.

12th July 1944: Moved to new position near Udler Bocad. Gerry mortaring, snipers active – Lt. Peters just missed bullet.

13th July 1944: Still same. Two tanks knocked out and our *(could be 'one')* tank overturned – two crew killed.

14th July 1944: Still mortaring and snipers still a nuisance. Went back to base for a rest.

15th July 1944: Moving to a position about 1 mile away, going to do patrols.

16th July 1944: In observation post – 6 Gerrys gave themselves up this morning.

17th July 1944 & 18th July 1944: *In margin:* Saw Tiger *and* 17th & 18th. Done Recce patrol to find enemy positions. Gerry fired at me and others (50 yds in front) and mortared us but lucky there was a pond. Wet but worth it.

19th July 1944: *In margin till 23rd July :* Garmont Area. Relieved Yanks, me and Gil set up an out post here today.
20th July 1944: Still firing at us – Gerry threw grenade at Sgt Dedman.
21st July 1944: At rest camp – taking it easy.
22nd July 1944: Still there. Visit beach, went to Paclam *(?)*
23rd July 1944: Returned to Position – Gerry still active.
24th July 1944: On out post again – Gerry shot Grumlish. *In margin is says 4T.*
25th July 1944: At harbour going out to STAND to position.
26th July 1944: Still at harbour, moved off in afternoon to the old position.
27th July 1944: Still same place. Gerry shot one of our chaps through the hand.
28th July 1944 & 29th July 1944: Went on patrol. 3 of us met two Gerry patrols – they threw grenades at us but lucky we are in a dip with spandoes.

(In the margin is the word HARDING *and two arrows pointing down toward the 30th July entry which is at the foot of the diary page.)*

30th July1944: Sniper and rifle fire followed by mortar, but got out – lucky. *(In the margin are the words* INFANTRY ATTACK.*)*
31st July 1944: Got near the Garmont area, Recce patrol near Villa Briorde.
1st August 1944: Recced for the Div attack, met stiff opposition 2 miles forward of there.
2nd August 1944: Yanks made attack with infantry – bags of prisoners started (?)
3rd August 1944: Still Recceing – found mortar sites – Cpl. Bater killed.
4th August 1944: In harbour waiting for orders. On Recce 2 miles from V Bocary.
5th August 1944: Back in reserve. Done Recce left of Villars Bocary.
6th August 1944: In reserve taking it easy.
7th August 1944: Still in reserve, taking it easy waiting for orders.
8th August 1944: Recce near V Bocary – now standing to for orders.
9th August 1944: Reserve again taking it easy.
10th August 1944: Moved to near the R. Orne in VB. Area brought in 6P.
11th August 1944: ON Recce nr same place, plenty of mortars, shells and spa*(ndoes).*
12th August 1944: Back at base – shell killed 1 chap, injured 2.
13th August 1944: Still at base in reserve.
14th August 1944: Moved to forward position on encirclement M.F.
15th August 1944: Same place – mortar time.
16th August 1944: Same place, mortar fix bombs. 56 Eggs moved out.
17th August 1944: In base waiting for big push.

1933 Diary ends here Dad must have got another one, in his letters he told his Mum he was using a diary from 1933 and asked her to get him another one perhaps she could only find one for 1942.

August 18th: Moved to Argentan??? For push with 11th Armoured brigade through the taped Gerrys route is through the Paris road, according to the higher ups we should not meet much opposition as he is supposed to be just about demoralised to give in, also they cannot have much arms left because of supplies being unable to reach them also I counted 56 lorry and half track knocked out and 6 tigers on the road.

Aug 19th: Moved forward again to post in Argintan??? In harbour waiting for orders carrier?? and arks?? out on recce also carrin??? Thinks we shall be moving tomorrow by the way the 11th Brigade are moving forward Yanks have crossed the Seine and bypassed Paris in the NW also 50 mile inland on the S France invasion.

August 20th: Pushed on today through the gap took 200 prisoners also plenty of vehicles have been knocked out round this area and bags of dead Gerry we are the first English boys the civvy have seen also prisoners are still coming in made advance of 20 – 30 m today took field hospital with wounded harbouring in woods for night.

August 21st: Pushed on again today plenty of prisoners we have passed through the town of Ruco les again first English they have seen got mobbed could not move for about 10 minutes came across blown up bridge had to send R.E. to lay down bridge waited until it was done then moved on again advanced 30 miles today in harbour nior/longd Vlmage. *(can't understand).*

Aug. 22nd: FALISE: I different harbour slept with 2 Gerry prisoners one pole the other German age 20 he says his father is fighting also that he has had nothing to eat, the Pole says he was forced by Gerry prisoner to fight would have nothing to do with him name is Joseph Gerrys name is Karl we fed them in morning and you would think they had nothing to eat for weeks.

Aug. 23rd: Moved back to base plenty of refugees round have found out that we are going to make a bridge C head over the seine, the people round here are very pleased with us also they gave us wine, eggs, and fruit spoke to women who could speak English she said that the Germans had thrown them out of their house and took it.

Aug. 24th: Still at same place the French woman who I spoke to yesterday was sleeping on straw with her children and husband gave them some fags and soap told us that the Germans allowed them 3 cigs a day if they work also they say soap is impossible to get have not had any for 2 years also Brewer is a larrd bord color ???

Aug 25th: Shifted to 2 miles of seine people are very nice went out and found Gerry barracks which had been abandoned also load of vehicles knocked out round here.

Think we are moving tomorrow and hope to get well across the seine so the say.

Aug 26th: Still at base have not moved yet plenty of aircraft active think we are moving tomorrow.

Aug 27th: Still at Base.

Aug 28th: (writing changed from ink to pencil) harder to read.

Moved to near Seine getting ready for a push toward the Belgium border think we shall move tomorrow went down village along the Seine got asked into a house by a man and his wife had Champagne cognac and also a few eggs from her she told us to come and see her again hope to go tomorrow came across big German Military barracks.

Aug 29th: Went to see the people near the seine again we had some champagne they have a business in Paris told us to come and spend our leave their if we get any also we could spend a holiday their after the war.

She gave me her address and also wanted us to stay the night but could not as we are moving tonight across the seine.

Aug 30th: Crossed the seine last night and now about 20mls inland.
Plenty of prisoners coming in about 100 taken today pushing on to Elbeuf We got to about 3 mile from there harbouring the night had a whiskey usher ???? also rum moving tomorrow a 4.30 Monty said in a message to us make every kilometre a bomb less for England.

Aug 31st: Pushed on again to near Amenis ? stayed there the night captured about 60 prisoners plenty of more dead about also have seen a B.B. sight. Heard that 5 have been taken today came across load of Gerry kit trucks, tanks lorry and horses also plenty of dead Gerrys round up some Gerry from woods.

Sept. 1st: Pushed on to near Ameins went out on Recce came across a camp with Tunss chaps captured in 1940 they had been their Guards prisoners and also a few more Gerry must be about 200 Gerry ..... funny chaps as the salute us and stand to attention also bags of Gerry kit here and lorries also officer quarters they had left plenty of kit.

Sept 2nd: Pushed on again to a place called Farrius got moved and every one in village came to see us the sang momalay and were very pleased to see us captured a good few Gerrys round here one a Sgt. Major and he cried his eyes out saw them in a corn field a burst off the bren soon brought them out.

Lille - Sept 3rd: Passed through Lille Gerry in some parts of it but not to much trouble got plenty of food drink off the French left Lille and every one all the way to Belgium are giving us stuff.
Went across the border into Belgium pushed on 10 miles and harboured the night in a field.
Passed by Pollen? Bridge yesterday saw all the Graves of English and Canadian.

Sept 4th: Pushed on again to Bercham came across Gerry convoy in flight knocked out 6 but was ordered to leave the rest and push on we went about 2 mile outside Beacham and came to Bridge what Gerry was trying to blow up so we had to guard it. The people are very nice here have had tea and other food in houses.

Sept 5th: Still at Bertram saw the free Belgium people set a collaborators house on fire also cut their hair and took them away.
We took some S.S. back to R.H.Q. and also the Villagers caught some more but before we knew they had strung them up.
Had tea in one of the local houses also taken to dance by the people at night.

Sept 6th: Still guarding Bridge – Anti tank Broked out 3 lorrys and one Tiger today.
Little activity expect to shift tonight to near Brussels shifted at 7 o clock to a place just outside Brussels went into the town by train had as much as we wanted of everything off the aws??.
Also met a girl named Evon.

Sept 7th: Shifted to other side of Brussells went there again at night still getting plenty to eat of off the people especially front ones also have been asked into the houses not much activity today met girl named Lorra found out the Air Born are being landed tonight.

Sept 8th: Shifted to the Albert Canal guarding a bridge Gerry mortaring and shelling it, a few prisoners taken today C Squadron and the 6 surrounded but later on Gerry forced to retreat, altogether he put in 14 counter attacks today, SS captured 2 carriers also crews.

Sept 9th: Still in same position Gerry patrols came across on Recce but turned back when coming in contact with our fire. Gerry mortars and shells still coming over also a few bombs dropped in the night. Plenty of refugees coming into our lines from Gerry side.

Sept 10th: Still at Canal position same as usual except a few shells.

Sept 11th: Shifted to Harbour going out on Recce tomorrow, things quiet in harbour.

Sept 14th: Still in same place, nothing doing today rained a lot but luckily we have some tents.

Sept 15th: Moved on to another Canal where we took up O.P. stayed very quiet but about 2 o'clock in morning there was quite a few Spondoes Fishing to see if there was any one on the other side we just kept low and let the bullets whim over our heads. Plenty of voices can be heard also vehicle movements.

Sept 16th: Still in same position can see Gerry walking about also 30 of them in a slit trench no more than 100 yards away wish we could fire but can not as it would let Gerry know that he was being observed and he must think no one is on the other side of Canal, saw a chap come up with bucket and bring food and mail also heard plenty of movement.

Sept 17th: Still in same position watched Gerry still messing around gave details of blown bridge to R.E. we left this position so that a barrage could be put down to allow the R.E to put up bridge, infantry crossed over the barrage and took up positions while the R.E made a bridge big push coming and going to push on the side sea.

Sept 18th: Now in corp grouping area watching for big push just been told by G.O. that Dempsy is very pleased with the 50th Recce work we have done and expect the counter attack we pause the key to staffing??? He also told us that we were 3 days ahead of the 7 Armoured corps and was waiting outside Vire for them.

Sept 19th: Still in base and waiting for big push –aby am??? We have been sent a personal message from Dempsy on the job done at Vire also for the 2000 prisoners taken in the Falaize gap.

Sept 20th: Still at base taking it easy expect to move tomorrow went out in the village tonight and had tea in a girls house, moving tomorrow.

Sept 21st: Moved at 4.30 in the morning to Holland went through to Andover to a place called Halover went out on Recce but things quiet a few vehicles knocked out here.

Sept 22nd: Still same position things quiet firing through the night but nothing else met a girl named ???

Sept 23rd: Shelled to where Gerry broke through but not much doing, plenty of shelling through the night.

Sept 24th: Shifted to the flank plenty of mortar fire shelling and spandos. A few Gerry prisoners taken today also woman.

Sept 25th: Still on the flank more prisoners taken Monty and Eisenhower also chief of the airborne stopped and spoke to us today, asked if we were getting our food ok also if there were any complaints he gave us 2500 fags between us and also told us we were being transferred from being called the 61st Recce to the 50th.

Sept 26th: Shifted to the Whellismi canal near Gerry on hill in front can see Germany from here I hope to be in there soon as the plan to go to the side sea has changed because of the bridges across the upper Rhine are blown so we are pushing west into Germany.

Sept 27th: Still in the same position not much to report only shelling and aircraft busy overhead met a girl who's address is: Annie Eloen, Kapelok C117. Beekin. Donk, Holland.

Sept 28th: Moved to harbour for rest before the next push which I hope will be the last push needed as Gerry can not last much longer or I hope not.

Sept 29th: Still in harbour waiting for further orders.

Sept 30th: Shifted to Mill out on recce saw the right Ark car that the O/C of a squadron got killed his name was major Alexandra also his grave rather quiet on recce nothing doing.

October 1st: Shifted to Nimagen passed over the bridge the first airborne captured, there is a hole in the Radig ?? bridge harboured the night in woods hope to be shifted tomorrow 50 of squadron allowed out to Nimigen so we tossed up but was not lucky.

October 2nd: Shifted to Armeins holding two railings??? Attack went in today Yanks and British plenty of fighting going on also plenty of bombs going over shelling and mortar 4 hrs heavy also a few spando active.

October 3rd: Still in same position we were relieved to go for baths first one since Beayeax came back to positions still the same as usual. Saw a dog fight while there Gerry is after the bridge but he got shot down and we saw the parachute.

October 4th: Still at the same position and hope to be moving tomorrow plenty of air activity also shelling and mortaring as I write this the sound of mortar shells air craft and machine gun fire can be heard.

(Colour of ink changed to black)

October 5th: Still in same position, hope to be moving tomorrow where I don't but things the same

October 6th: Moved to Arnhem prisoners are only 15 yrs old with about 6 weeks service in. Plenty of spando fire our guns have been firing all the time we are with the Yank airborne.

October 7th: Still at Arnhem east of it Gerry put in 4 counter attacks today also plenty of shelling. We are with the Yank air born they are a fine lot of chaps plenty of mortar fire and shelling also a few air craft about.

October 8th: Still the same two counter attacks today also shelling which has increased.

October 9th: Still the same out on recce quiet.

October 10th: In harbour about a mile away from positions.

October 11th: Move to a place called Warle near a dyke made friends with a girl named Annie plenty of 77I round this way they have been patrolling the dyke also some princess Greens?? troops here.

October 12th: Moved to the end of town went and saw the girls I know had tea there also some drinks and a bunch of grapes. They are funny people in the day they call every one Tommies at night they are scarred as anything and everything they have they call mophs *(can't understand last few words).*

October 13th: Still the same position on forward O.P. directing artillery fire on Gerry O.Ps a bit of action through night.

October 14th: Still same place went to house again for tea. Gerry fired at the church tower today and brought it down some of our chaps in stores troop were up there luckily the first one hit the church low, they only got a bit of shrapnel in them. Lucky they did not get more.

October 15th: Still at Wannel taking it easy made a few more friends went to the girls house again things quiet.

October 16th: Moved from Wannel to a place called Vvoo near Elst near Arnhem on reserve at the moment plenty of shells knocking about.

October 17th: Still in reserve about 4 Gerry tiger tanks knocked out round here also as active as yesterday the shells.

October 18th: Still in the same place in reserve.

October 19th: Still in reserve going into position tomorrow I think.

October 20th: (In pencil) Shifted tonight to the other side of Arnhem Gerry 100 yds away only 25y one was a few grenades etc.

October 21st: Cut on out post tonight Gerry throwing Grenades over our positions and plenty of Spando fire but otherwise quiet can see Gerry walking about also his O.P.

October 22nd: On out post tonight Gerry came behind us a small patrol of 10 men roughly I noticed them and shouted Halt who goes there when they were 25 yards away and they were 10 yards away when they stopped I wasn't half scared but they only opened up with Smisy and our Bren gun and grenades soon got rid of them.

October 23rd: Still in same position CDL Slack went away as he got hurt from last nights do but I think he will be okay.

October 24th: Still in same position and taking it easy I think.

October 25th: Still same place plenty of Gerry dead round here.

October 26th: Still same place.

October 27th: Still same place.

October 28th: Still same place.

October 29th: Still taking it easy.

October 30th: Still same position.

October 31st: Went to Antwerp today have been relieved by Yank Air Born.

November 1st: In Antwerp having a good time.

November 2nd: In Antwerp.

November 3rd: In Antwerp.

November 4th: Back at Base taking it easy had good news about Antwerp.

November 5th: Back at Base.

November 6th: Moved to Zetlon on O.P plenty of Spando fire also shelling and mortar.

November 7th: Still on O.P.

November 8th: Still on O.P.

November 9th: Still on O.P.

November 10th: Still on O.P.

November 15th: On forward O.P on the River Patrol floating about behind us somewhere saw two chaps crawling so we changed our position blooming cold tonight plenty of Spando fire etc. LER is the name of the river over??? Arnhem.

November 16th: Moved to Base at Venssen in a civvy house.

November 17th: Still at same place taking it easy.

November 18th: (Blue Pen) Moored in a position Bernal near Arnhem about the coldest and wettest position I have ever been in. There is 2ft of water in the slit trenches and we have to stand in it 3 chaps went ill tonight I recon I shall have had it if I stay here. Plenty of Spando fire.

November 19th: Still same place and plenty of water also Gerry shelling and mortar also Spando the INFANTRY sappers laid a minefield tonight.

November 20th: Still in the same and things are still bad another 2 chaps went ill I feel pretty bad all the chaps feel the same the infantry are still laying mines one chap dropped one and got his foot blown off the shrapnel just missed us.

November 21st: Still the same moving into burnt house making it strong point Gerry shelled us with his 210 a bit of shrapnel hit my tin hat and ricocheted off. Just missing Cpl. Heady Grey I was bending down in the slit trench.

November 22nd: Moved into the house it just like a luxury as bad as it is Gerry still active and also plenty of mortars.

November 23rd: Still the same.

November 24th: Still the same.

November 25th: Still the same saw flying bomb.

November 26th: Still the same.

November 27th: Still the same.

November 28th: Still the same.

November 29th: Still the same.

November 30th: Still the same.

December 1st: Gerry started to flood the area the water has risen 2ft many Gerrys trapped.

December 2nd: Water still rising Gerry blew another dam last night and the place is quite bad many Gerrys gave their selves up because the flooding had trapped them they are nearly all air force chaps.

December 3rd: Moved today to Mill got relived by the 59th spent the night in a café all of us been??? for supper.

December 4th: Still same place.

December 5th: Moved to Ell near weet in a civvy's house having a good time.

December 6th: Same place.

December 9th: Same place.

December 10th: Moved to ell relived the 53rd on forward O.P overlooking the mass??? to a good position.

Diary comes to an end.

Under January 27th is Dads brother Bobs address as follows: -
CFM B O Brewer, No 6019180, Attached 537.SL, R A Battery. Danbury, Essex

Under January 29th is Dads address
14631319, Tpr Eric Brewer, Mount Battle Troop, A Squadron, Combined Recce T C, Menin Lines Catterick Camp, York

Under January 25th is Kens address Dads eldest brother
W/O K J Brewer, No 581436, The Sgts mess, RAF, Killadean, Mt Eniskillen, C/O Fermanaugh Nth Ireland

January 26th another address
W Brown C/X 374092, Mess 25/4, H.M.S. Tobot 3, C/O PO Box Robourgh, Nr Plymouth, Devon

I don't know who this is.

Photographs of Tpr. Eric Brewer with comrades –
Cpl. Polwin, L.Cpl. Slack, Tpr.'s Tilly (squirrel) & Dillon.

ORDER OF THE DAY

BY LIEUTENANT COLONEL P.H.A. BROWNRIGG, DSO
COMMANDING 61ST RECONNAISSANCE REGIMENT, ROYAL ARMOURED CORPS.
MONDAY 5TH FEBRUARY 1945

Today after three and a half years existence and nearly eight months continuous service, the Regiment is breaking up.

The break up is due to one cause only, to the conversion of our Division, the 50th (Northumbrian) – resulting from the heavy casualties sustained – into a training Division in England. This conversion left us like orphans; for a time we continued to work as an independent Recce Regiment, but though two formations were anxious to have our services, it was decided that with the Army so short of men, it could not afford a spare Regiment, however good. This decision was made by the C-in-C himself, with great regret, after two appeals by Lt-General Horrocks, Commander 30 Corps, and two appeals by Maj-Gen Graham, Commander 50 (N) Division.

Though for ourselves it is a very hard blow, we have the comfort of knowing that we served the finest Division of the British Army, for the most critical months of the war and made the Division almost as proud of us as we were of the Division; and we know too that when Runstedt threatened to break right through the American and British Armies, our Regiment was called on, first to help hold the line, and then to prepare the counter-offensive. So well did the Regiment acquit itself in the Ardennes that at the end of the operation the Corps Commander motored 40 miles through snow and ice to congratulate and thank you. Our losses during this last episode in our history have been:- Killed 48 – Wounded 144 – Missing 23.

So we finish our history with our name and reputation higher than they have ever been. In achieving this record many of our friends have lost their lives and many more have been wounded. It is a heavy price but to set against it, the Regiment has accounted for at least 5,000 of the enemy, of whom 4,000 have been made prisoner. Without doubt many of the others that we have not seen have been killed and wounded by our mortars. The balance is well on our side. This result is due in great measure to the founder of the Regiment. Lt-Col Sir William Mount, Bart. TD. To him we owe our training and our fine Regimental spirit. Many of us have found in this Regiment a greater comradeship than we knew either before the war or in other Regiments. When we break up, let our contingents take with them that spirit to their new Regiments. In doing so, though our history is finished. I believe that you will continue to add honour to our name.

Good luck to all of you, and thank you for your magnificent work. May we meet again.

P H A Brownrigg (Lt-Col)

RECCE VICTORIA CROSS

On 18th August 1944 at St. Lambert Sur Dives, Major V. Currie, 29th Canadian Armoured Reconnaissance Regiment, won the Victoria Cross; "For 36 hours, beat off repeated counter attacks, finally capturing the Normandy village."

THE CANADIAN ARMY

The official citation reads as follows: -
The King has been graciously pleased to approve the award of the VICTORIA CROSS to: -
Major David Vivian Currie
29th Canadian Armoured Reconnaissance Regiment. (South Alberta Regt.)

In Normandy on 18th August 1944, Major Currie was in command of a small mixed force of Canadian tanks, self – propelled anti-tank guns and infantry which was ordered to cut off the main escape routes from the Falaise pocket.

This force was held up by strong enemy resistance in the village of St. Lambert Sur Dives, and two tanks were knocked out by 88mm guns. Major Currie immediately entered the village alone on foot at last light through the enemy outposts to reconnoitre the German defences and to extricate the crews of the disabled tanks which he succeeded in doing in spite of heavy mortar fire.

Early the following morning, without any previous artillery bombardment, Major Currie personally led an attack on the village in the face of fierce opposition from enemy tank guns and infantry, and by noon had succeeded in seizing and consolidating a position half way inside of the village.

During the next thirty-six hours the Germans hurled one counter attack after another against the Canadian Force but so skillfully had Major Currie organised his defensive position that these attacks were repulsed with severe casualties to the enemy after heavy fighting.

At dusk on the 20th August the Germans attempted to mount a final assault on the Canadian positions but the attacking Force was routed before it could even be deployed. Seven enemy tanks, twelve 88mm guns and forty vehicles were destroyed, three hundred Germans were killed, five hundred wounded and two thousand one hundred captured. Major Currie then promptly ordered an attack and completed the capture of the village thus denying the Chambois-Trun escape route to the remnants of two German armies cut off in the Falaise pocket.

Throughout three days and nights of fierce fighting Major Currie's gallant conduct and contempt for danger set a magnificent example to all ranks of the Force under his command.

On one occasion he personally directed the fire of his command tank onto a tiger tank, which had been harassing his position and succeeded in knocking it out. During another attack while the guns of his command tank were taking on other targets at longer ranges, he used a rifle from the turret to deal with individual snipers who had infiltrated to within fifty yards of his Headquarters. The only time reinforcements were able to get through to his Force he himself led the forty men forward into their positions and explained the importance of their task as a part of the defence, when during the next attack these new reinforcements withdrew under the intense fire brought down by the enemy, he personally collected them and led them forward into position again where inspired by his leadership they held for the remainder of the battle. His employment of the artillery support, which became available after his original attack went in, was typical of his cool calculation of the risks involved in every situation. At one time, despite the fact that short rounds were falling within fifteen yards of his own tank, he ordered fire from medium artillery to continue because of its devastating effect upon the attacking enemy in his immediate area.

Throughout the operations the casualties to Major Currie's Force were heavy. However, he never considered the possibility of failure or allowed it to enter the minds of his men. In the words of one of his non-commissioned officers, "We knew at one stage that it was going to be a fight to the finish but he was so cool about it, it was impossible for us to get excited". Since all the officers under his command were either killed or wounded during the action, Major Currie had virtually no respite from his duties and in fact obtained only one hour's sleep during the entire period. Nevertheless, he did not permit his fatigue to become apparent to his troops and throughout the action took every opportunity to visit weapon pits and other defensive posts to talk to his men, to advise them as to the best use of their weapons and to cheer them with words of encouragement. When his Force was finally relieved and he was satisfied that the turnover was complete he fell asleep on his feet and collapsed.

There can be no doubt that the success of the attack on and stand against the enemy at St. Lambert Sur Dives can largely be attributed to this officer's coolness, inspired leadership and skillful use of the limited weapons at his disposal.

The courage and devotion to duty shown by Major Currie during a prolonged period of heavy fighting were out-standing, and had a far-reaching effect on the successful outcome of the battle.

St. LAMBERT-SUR-DIVES AUGUST 18th 1944

1. *"Germans surrendering to Major D.V. Currie's Force. Major Currie himself, tired and grimy appears at the left, pistol in hand. This is as close as we are ever likely to come to a photograph of a man winning the Victoria Cross." – C.P. Stacey. The Victory Campaign.*
2. *Major Currie standing in front of a Sherman tank in Normandy.*

REUNION DOWN UNDER (DECEMBER 1982)

(Newsletter Old Comrades Association)

Dennis Dolby and Roy Howard (both 'A' Sqdn.) hold mini-reunion in Adelaide, South Australia, and open up the beer to drink a health to all comrades of TT41. A typical reminder of the long lasting friendships engendered by the spirit of 61 Recce:

A happy outcome of the lasting friendship was the kind co-operation of Dennis and Marguerite Dolby upon the arrival of Roy's elder son John and his wife in Adelaide on 18th May, 1977. They were met at the airport by Dennis and family – and who carried who home after the evening's jollity is nobody's business. Furthermore, Dennis's son-in law gave John an old car. A period of 'stables' by this younger generation, and John and wife soon played havoc with the Adelaide traffic under command of Corporal Dolby. Dennis is now scratching around for more straw for the palliasses and stocking up the cellar.... no kidding. Roy deeply appreciates the kindness of Dennis, Marguerite and family.

We will no doubt be hearing more from Roy Howard at a later date when he and Edna have made a visit to inspect billets and latrines etc.

E.T.A. given, Christmas 1982 and mission accomplished. Still a dab hand with the map reading it seems!   *Ed. TT41*

Roy Howard & Dennis Dolby 'A' Sqdn. (Adelaide, South Australia 1982)

POET'S CORNER

THE D-DAY MEN - William George Seger

Did you sail to France with me,
In that exclusive company,
When with Neptune we held sway,
To honour a date now called D Day?

Did you feel as sick as I,
Hoping that you'd quickly die,
Before you reached that distant shore,
So that you would not suffer more?

Did you pray as ramps went down,
That you would not slip and drown,
Before you'd had a chance to see
The fields and towns of Normandy?

Did you curse the 'compo' grub,
As you got your slit trench dug,
And wouldn't you have sold your head
For a slice or two of English bread?

ACHTUNG MINEN the notice read,
Did you walk in others tread,
And were you happy when you pitched
Headfirst into that wayside ditch?

To escape the moaning minnies blast,
Hoping each would be the last,
And didn't you want to shout hooray,
At having survived the LONGEST DAY?

If you nod and agree with me,
On all these ancient memories,
Put it there Pal without any fuss,
Enough to know you're one of us.

Ours is the glory and the pride,
No matter how the youngsters chide,
Stick out your chest as far as you can,
And shake hands with another D DAY MAN

OBITUARIES

OBITUARY: - (8TH MAY 1972)

Regimental Sergeant Major J. Lunn. (Regt. HQ) *(Newsletter Old Comrades Association)*

Mr. Lunn joined the Regiment on its formation, and his Seaforth Highland attire on his arrival gave rise to his becoming known, behind locked doors, as 'Angus' – a non-de-plume he was to become remembered by for evermore, coupled with the still-echoing call "here boy!"

By virtue of his rank, it would be unusual to say that Mr Lunn was a popular figure, but he was completely fair and he played the major part in welding the many contingents from diverse regiments into the highly disciplined 61 Recce. The tale is still told of his first fireside chat to the Regiment:- "We are all on trial and anybody who isn't satisfactory is going back. This includes me – but **I'm** not going back!" He treated one and all alike - a'feared from Commanding Officers down to Sanitary Operators, and anyone with a guilty conscience (who hadn't) avoided his path via first escape hatch. He could however, be a friend on or off duty, as Reg Harper writes:- "As one who got to know him very well, he was definitely not as black as he was painted by a long way (even if I did get the rough edge of his tongue on many an occasion) and a lot of good deeds he did were unnoticed by many." And an ex-Squadron Commander writes "There is little doubt that Mr Lunn's fearsome inculation of discipline during our long period of training and waiting saved many lives when we finally got into action as TT41."

His passing leaves a great gap in the Regiment, but he will be remembered to the last man. He had a tough job instilling discipline (including the lying-in-wait 23.59 hrs) but he controlled us and despite the rough edge of his tongue quoted by Reg, we cannot fail but look back in respect for Mr Lunn as a strict but kind father. When seen a few years ago, Mr Lunn assured that he remembered all 'his boys' and was proud of their success and credit to the Regiment. In return, the greatest compliment the Regiment pays is that if it should all happen again, the cry would be – "Come back, Angus – All is forgiven!"

Ed. TT41

OBITUARY: - (18TH DEC 1976)

Major E E (Tony) Macotta. (Regt. HQ) *(Newsletter Old Comrades Association)*

From the moment he joined 'B' Squadron in Northern Ireland, as John Cave recalls, from a smart Cavalry Regiment in a British Warm with an astrakhan collar, it was clear that we had acquired a remarkable and loveable character. It was fortunate for us that the hatches on British tanks were not constructed for soldiers of Tony's shape, and so they let him come to us.

Outwardly ill equipped to a parade ground soldier he had all the qualities for a first class Staff Officer. With his quick and sensitive brain, unfailing good humour with a wonderful laugh that began deep in his belly, superb bridge playing, and appreciation of good food and drink and ability to find them in unlikely places, it was no surprise that he was summoned before very long for duty at RHQ. He was Colonel Mount's Adjutant for the invasion. The extremely complicated and special organisation required for our two invasion roles in no way daunted Tony. The Regiment had to be re-shaped with special equipment. A and B Squadrons plus RHQ, all at about 40% of normal strength, were to land on D-Day from about H plus 4 onwards, join up with 8th Armoured Brigade, and on D + 1 occupy the high ground near Villers Bocage miles inland and hold it for four or five days until 2nd Army caught up with us.

C Sqdn had to provide special signals contact patrols with the main assault battalions of 50th Division. Thereafter the rear echelon would arrive from England and the whole Regiment would be re-established. Naturally, these things didn't happen as planned but this was no fault of Tony's meticulous Staff Duties.

While Tony was with our rear echelon in England, he typically (and probably illegally) managed to tune into the 61 Recce net on D + 2, soon after the Regiment had started the rush to Villers Bocage, he heard the dread words from Colonel Mount's Operator. 'My Sunray has been hit.' Through an Uncle in the War Office he found that the CO had been taken to a hospital in Birmingham, and was able to give Lady Mount the first and comparatively reassuring news of the CO's condition.

There was great rejoicing when Tony and the other stalwarts from England joined the Regiment in France. Tony's personality made almost any HQ a place of cheer, and he continued to be a superb Adjutant until Major Alexander's death on the road to Nijmegan led to Tony being promoted to take over HQ Squadron. All my memories of Tony are good: this bullion broker had a heart of gold although he could be goaded into a crisp riposte. I think it was when Gunner Thorne twitted him 'Of all people having such a dull pewter signet ring' that he snapped "Pewter – its platinum, you bloody fool!" Much of his time and energy after the war he gave up to Jewish clubs in the East End and no good cause ever came to him in vain. Never, I believe during the war, did Tony show any sign of fear. It was typical of him that he did not opt, as he easily could have, for a much safer and more comfortable form of war; but I think he admitted that he didn't particularly relish the thought of being captured. What a man to have with you in war – and in peace. Indeed a great and loveable man. Our deepest sympathy goes to his widow and family.

Philip Brownrigg

OBITUARY: - (23RD JAN 1981) *(Newsletter Old Comrades Association)*

Sergeant Joe (Doc) Jarvis. SB. St. J. (Regt. HQ)

Joe had a long Regimental history – honourable TA service 5th Manchester Rgt: 1920, possessor of the Territorial Efficiency Medal and three Clasps.

He was also a Serving Brother of St. John 1915-1963, retiring as Superintendent, Tyldesley Branch. In Recce days at Ashridge, he instituted the First Aid Class under our Medical Officer, Dr. McGlone, to ensure that every man had such knowledge before action. Transferred to us from the Manchester Regiment as our medical sergeant, Joe served with 61 Recce throughout its existence, following on as a loyal member of the OCA together with his life-long interest in the Royal British Legion. For many years he paid our Tribute to 'Absent Friends'. Perhaps his zenith was the Last Post Menin Gate Ceremony when his rendering of the Citation drew high tribute from our Iseghem Comity and other Belgian friends in attendance: as Rafael said on their behalf 'Doc Jarvis was superb......' and indeed honoured by Iseghem in the award of the Brandweer Golden Medal. We will remember them, as Doc would pronounce. To our sorrow, Joe himself is gone, and we who are left will be remembering in 1981 and years to come.

Ed. TT41

OBITUARY: - (12TH DEC 1982) *(Newsletter Old Comrades Association)*

Major Stewart Johnson. (Regt. HQ)

The Major originally served in the Worcestershire Regiment TA and commanded 183 Anti-tank Troop. He served in 61 Recce throughout its formation becoming well known as O.C. 'B' Sqdn, of which he took command in January 1944. To allow Major Johnson to undertake a Special Duty as liaison officer in January, Major Harding took over command, however, on 12th June 1944 Major Johnson was appointed Second in Command of the Regiment upon Colonel Brownrigg taking command of the Regiment after Sir William was wounded. It is believed that the Major was posted to 43rd Recce on our disbandment. Major Johnson is recalled as a highly respected and efficient officer by all who knew him.

Ed. TT41

OBITUARY: - (3RD JUNE 1981) *(Newsletter Old Comrades Association)*

Major Frank Harding. MC. 'B' Squadron.

Frank, Mrs Harding wrote, always held the Reconnaissance Regiment in great affection and, in a strange way, considered his time in the Regiment as some of the best years of his life. And indeed he held great affection for the OCA too – a staunch supporter attending dinners more or less regularly until 1970 when minor illness afterwards prevented him (apart from his last attendance in 1977). And one does not forget his co-operation when called upon – the willingness to Speak at Dinners at a moments notice or the occasional emergency, and his speech for the Official Reception at the 1974 Iseghem Visit. Frank also had poetic qualities – he humbly rejected himself as a recognised poet, his attempts at verse being ways to recollect....particularly the times spent together in the 61st Recce..... putting into poetic metre things still close to the heart. In 1959 he circulated what he called a hotch-pot of verse titled 'War Intervened and Other Poems'. Many of these with others he duly comprised in his 'War Echoes Over Thirty Years,' published in 1970. He will always be remembered by his 'Hardingites' and others who knew him. From Sir William... "most sorry....a splendid chap and most helpful to me during the long periods of training in Northern Ireland." And an appreciation of Frank from Colonel Brownrigg also at some length.

N.B. – *Several of Major Hardings poems from 'War Echoes etc:' are reproduced within these pages.*

OBITUARY:- (30TH OCT 1984) *(Newsletter Old Comrades Association)*

Max Murphy. 'B' Squadron

Originally in the Air Training Corps 1941 with ambition to become a 'tail-end Charlie', and following medical and educational tests, he was to go home and wait – Still waiting 1943 when Recce called, joining at Gallowgate Camp North Yorkshire, then off to 1 Recce Training Camp Scarborough and Christmas dinner 1943 with 61 Recce at Shornecliffe....and throughout.

Max was a frequent contributor to the letter pages and book review columns of the Huddersfield 'Examiner', and also a local broadcaster. In the early 60's he wrote a script for the pilot TV series which was to turn Harry Worth into a household name. During the 70's he worked as a Press Officer for the Oxfam Waste-saver Scheme in Kirklees and also compiled a series of articles for the Yorkshire Holiday Guide, such was his range of local knowledge.

He wrote several items for the Old Comrades Association Newsletter over the years, and was a frequent member at our reunions.

N.B. – Max Murphy's last job was as Feature Editor (Northern Division) of the Illustrated County Magazine Group.

OBITUARY: - (10th Oct 1973) *(Newsletter Old Comrades Association)*

Captain Joe Meredith. M.B.E.

An appreciation by Major E.E. Foley Rayer. ('A' Squadron Commander)

Joe Meredith came of an old Worcestershire family, which had farmed at Chaddesley Corbett for several generations. In 1938 he saw that his duty was to join, like many of us, the TA; in his case it was the 7th Bn. The Worcestershire Regiment. He went to France with the Battalion in 1939 and was commissioned into the 9th Bn of that Regiment in 1940.

Having been posted to the Brigade Anti-tank Company (182 Inf. Bde.) he was one of the original officers selected by Lt.-Col. Sir W.M. Mount for service with the newly formed 61st Divisional Reconnaissance Regiment in 1941. He was appointed Transport Officer, which appointment he held until 1944 when he took over the duties of Technical Adjutant and played an important part in the organisation of the water-proofing of vehicles in preparation for D-Day.

Kind and gentle, and a friend to all, Joe Meredith leaves a sad gap in the lives and memories of many of us. He was affectionately known to all ranks throughout the Regiment, as 'Towrope' because of his duties in connection with the recovery of vehicles lost to us through breakdown or through enemy action.

N.B. – *Captain Meredith was awarded the British Empire Medal.*

Major Rayer lost a leg when he stepped on an anti-personnel mine on 'The Island' in Holland during the advance towards Arnhem.

OBITUARY: - (SEPT 1977) *(Newsletter Old Comrades Association)*

Colonel Frederick Gough. MC, TD. (1st Airborne Reconnaissance Sqn.)

A man to be greatly admired and to whom 61 Recce pay their respects on his passing.

Strong association with the Territorial Army and London Rifle Brigade 1924 and 1939. Fought in Finland against Russia and a member of the famous 5th Battn Scots Guards formed for ski-ing duties in Finland. Served with GHQ France, and after Dunkirk, the Colonel became one of the original members of the 1st Airborne Division as a Commander of its Reconnaissance unit with action in North Africa 1943 and successful landing at Taranto Italy, for which he was awarded the Military Cross. Taken prisoner at Arnhem 1944, escaped April 1945 to join the Americans in Bavaria. He rejoined the TA in 1947. Memorial service was held in St Martins-in-the-Fields London, 27/01/78.

OBITUARY:- (6TH JAN 1985) *(Newsletter Old Comrades Association)*

END OF AN ERA

General Sir Brian Horrocks. KCB, KBE, DSO, MC.

One of Britains greatest World War 2 Commanders, and a former Black Rod of the House of Lords, and well known presenter of the TV Series – World at War. A driving force behind success in North Africa, he went on to play a leading part in the defeat of Germany before retiring from the army in 1949. He then went into television forging a new career as an interpreter of famous wartime battles, among them the miracle of Dunkirk, the holocaust of the Battle of Stalingrad and the invasion of Europe from the Normandy beach-heads, - talking calmly and objectively about events in which he himself had had a leading part. It was his war wounds - received while a corps commander in North Africa – which forced him to retire from the Army and according to his friend, Reuter Chairman Sir Dennis Hamilton, Sir Brian never fully recovered, adding that there was still metal in his body when he died. Sir Brian had been seriously ill for about a year. Some time passed, our Pete Hussey visited Sir Brian who later was invited to attend our Reunion – due to ill health, Sir Brian was unable to attend, nevertheless sending good wishes to the 61st Recce. As a unit within 30 Corps, and under command of Sir Brian, Colonel Brownrigg specially had operational contact, and of his recollections and in personal tribute to Sir Brian, Colonel Brownrigg writes: -

"We of 61 Recce owe a tremendous debt to General Horrocks. Not only did we, like the rest of 30 Corps, profit from his superb leadership and tactical mastery, but we also gained a new, though comparatively brief, lease of life from his intervention on our behalf. As Old Comrades know, 'Jorrocks' was a great supporter of 61 Recce, and once told the assembled regiment that he had never seen a better action than the one we had just carried out on the left flank of the Corps. When we were in Iseghem in 1944, the decision was made to break up the 50th Division and we started the gloomy process of the disbandment of TT41. With little hope of success, I set off to see General Horrocks at Corps HQ while he was conducting the early stages of the assault on the Rhine. The General saw me at once, telephoned 'Monty' in my presence, and told him that our regiment was being broken up and what a dreadful mistake this was. "They would be worth a Brigade to me," he said. As a result we were re-formed and took, I think, a valuable part in the Ardennes campaign. It is true that the axe fell finally after that, but I am certain that those of us who survived never lost a particle of our admiration and affection for this very great man."

P.H.A. Brownrigg.

(Let us now praise famous men and our fathers that begat us....) Ecclesiasticus IX.2.

OBITUARY: - (14TH JULY 1987) *(Newsletter Old Comrades Association)*

Corporal Ronnie Washburn. 'A' Squadron

Ron suffered a very serious head injury in a Normandy action on the 4th, August 1944 from which he never fully recovered physically or mentally but plodded on courageously, ... 'Can't do what I should like but not a worry I suppose!' he would write. Friends, however, well knew his up-and-down days and were pleased, when due to his deteriorating health, that he was accommodated in a British Legion Home. Ron served with 61 Recce throughout – a most popular and well liked figure, his kind disposition and humour never failing to bring a smile to all who had the good fortune to know him, and his passing, like Les Eldridge and many others, leaves a gap in the lives of many. Ron attended Normandy '69 and several Reunions up to 1976 after which his health prevented the travelling. The service was held at Napton-on-the-hill Church, Rugby. The Regiment was represented by Alf Bedlow, Joe Duddy, Ernest & Nora Brobbin, Ron Burford, Arthur Davy, Wilf, Vera and John Dawson, Les & Celia Foot, Frank & Joyce Hampton, Roy & Edna Howard, Reg & Renee Jackson and Fred Lane. A floral tribute in 61 Recce colours was presented on behalf of the Regiment OCA. A most appropriate Service was conducted by the Vicar of Napton Parish – Rev. Peter Jackson, and what better and true Tribute to be made: "He was a gentle man...." The cortege then proceeded about 11 miles to the short Cremation Service at Oakley Wood Crematorium, and then all proceeded to Leamington Spa for a fine buffet arranged by Alan & Mrs Bennett – allowing this handful of Old Comrades a mini-reunion in honour of Ron.

Alan & Mrs Bennett (Ron's sister) were very moved by the special contingent of old comrades of the 61st Recce and wrote in appreciation of the kindness shown by many, either in attendance or condolence letters: 'On behalf of all Ron's Family I would like to say a sincere thank you to you and to all Old Comrades who attended, in spite of the obvious sadness of the occasion, it was a pleasure to meet so many, and of great comfort to his family to know that Ron was held in such high regard. We can appreciate now what a great bunch of chaps he served with and why he looked forward to the reunions while he was able to do so and why it meant so much to him to keep in touch with so many of his former comrades. I would be pleased if you could include this letter in your next Newsletter as I would be unable to write to everyone who attended or wrote to us individually. We trust that 61 Recce will continue to enjoy many happy reunions in the future. Once again grateful thanks to you all. With kind regards, yours sincerely, Alan Bennett.....'

Thank you Alan and Mrs Bennett and for interest in wishing to remain in touch with our Association. Ron may have suffered some confusion in present day matters, but he *never forgot detail* of his Recce days or friends....

Ed. TT41

PERSONAL FROM WILF DAWSON

Once again with the blessing of the chairman I take his perch this time to thank the many who have extended kind thoughts towards me during the year.... If at the risk of becoming a bore `cos its all about I.

As one of humble and retiring nature, a pleasant if embarrassing spotlight glare at the April Reunion with the honour of receiving the Izagem Brandweer Golden Medal and Diploma from Marcel on behalf of the Brandweer, Town and people. A token of their gratitude presented to me but perhaps a symbol of the Town's gratitude to the Regiment for its part played in the Liberation.....And as such, an Award I shall always treasure on each behalf.

Further surprises, this time from the OCA, at my Office Retirement Party in July. The general run of cards and what's this – OCA 61 Recce: famous names springing forth. Apparently all secret at Dinner 79 but how.... Just the night I didn't have ears to the ground. Thank you all very much for the signed missive to accompany shoulder flashes.

Not that this was the only surprise of the evening for as the troops came marching in – surely not – can't be – Colonel Brownrigg! Recce may rarely be out of mind but I must admit that on this particular evening with build-up worse than any reunion night, my old CO was well in the wilds! Like one of those Max Murphy mixed up army dreams, kit bag lost and all that. However, no dream and a great honour to me for the Colonel to be present especially on this the hottest day of the year and casting aside any transport assistance offered by secret LOs. A memorable day in anyone's turn – more so to me with 61 Recce well and truly represented.

Then joining the Retirement Regiment soon to be round MO Hut. Months of sciatica gippo brightened with OCA signals. SQMS Wade whipping 252s (one of them without friends?) For unauthorised removal of doors and jeopardising Sec duties; Major Wortley dishing Severe Reps for absence from All-Hallows; Bernard Gilkes along with Rolfe, Wacko and Millso (and Wadey again) on net detailing 0630 hrs run-walks; Les Foot recommending Tankerville Bridge jog; Percy Barker warning to stop quick drags in the bathroom like he had to....never ending list all adding up to how Reg Mills would put it; you have all been what the White Cliffs of Dover were to Britain in the darkest days.

With the sciatica lark easing up, the wisdom tooth saga follow-on should be rectified by Field General in April then perhaps I can return to the solitude of humble back room.

In the meantime, thank you all for the kind thoughts,

Back to your sections,

Best wishes,
Wilf Dawson.

Never argue with your doctor – he has inside information!

OBITUARY: - (10TH MARCH 1988) *(Newsletter Old Comrades Association)*

A tribute from his two 61 Recce Regt. C.O.'s Lt.-Col. Sir William Mount Bart. DSO, TD. & Lt.-Col. P.H.A. Brownrigg CMG, DSO, OBE, TD.

Wilf Dawson. 'A' Squadron

Wilf Dawson had been putting his careful finishing touches to the Newsletter on Friday, February 26th. As he was tired, he went to bed at 9.30 p.m., and when Vera went to see him half an hour later, he had died. He had almost literally worked himself to death in his self-allotted and very valuable task of preserving and nourishing 61 Recce O.C.A. Two years earlier his doctor had warned him that he should give up this arduous responsibility, but apart from his family, this was his life, and he kept resolutely on, spending his energy and, as we now learn, his own money on this operation.

He took on the organisation of the annual reunion in 1960, and in 1967, when still a pillar of the Post Office, he started the Newsletter. Wilf always set himself the highest standards, and the Newsletter was so well written and edited that he could easily have been a successful journalist.

When he retired from the Post Office in 1979, he gave his extra time to 61 Recce. He somehow managed to know of illnesses and other problems among our Old Comrades, and was constantly writing letters of encouragement and sometimes visiting, and persuading other Comrades to do the same. Between the two of us, we would probably have 50 telephone calls and as many letters from Wilf each year: - 'A' had had an operation; 'B's wife was in hospital; 'C' was having a difficult financial time owing to an accident and Wilf was getting him help from R.A.C. Benevolent Fund. Besides all this work he was the major organiser of the Reconnaissance Corps Remembrance Day Service at All Hallows.

Less than a week after Wilf's death, one of us had a telephone call from Australia from our Old Comrade, Dennis Dolby, who had somehow heard the news. His emotion and grief came through clearly on the line. The attendance at Wilf's funeral was proof that 61 Recce Old Comrades were determined to put on record what they owed to Wilf and their deep sympathy with Vera and John.

We know indeed the great sorrow that Vera and John are suffering, but they must have been much comforted and deeply moved by the crowd of heartfelt tributes to Wilf, and by all those, including our good friends from Belgium, who travelled long distances to pay their respects and give their thanks at the funeral. We know, too, how much Vera and John contributed to Wilf's work.

Wilf had been a most valuable, respected and popular member of 61 Recce from its formation until his very severe wound at Briquessard brought his active service with the Regiment to an end. For some years before his death he suffered from heart disease, but in no way did he allow this to lesson his efforts and his concern for 61 Recce and all his Old Comrades.

What a true and wonderful Comrade.

William Mount. Phillip Brownrigg.

THE LAST SCENE OF ALL

(Newsletter Old Comrades Association)

TOMORROW'S WORLD AT LARGE – BBC 1 – 1st September 1982

In this broadcast, our Reg Mills, was expected to be participating in a Geriatric Programme. There is some disappointment that Reg's contribution was not included – nevertheless an auntie, Mrs Nelly Potter, one of the elderly in the geriatric ward, was seen – a spirited lady who when chided by the nurse for not rising from bed, replied firmly "I am not going to get up because I don't want to live, I don't want to go anywhere, except in a box." Soon after the film was completed she got her wish.

The programme dealt with several cases of geriatric problems - in some ways a glaring advertisement for euthanasia. What is the point of living on after senile dementia has set in? What purpose......when medical staff state 'Most of them have no sense of their own dignity'. But there are moments of hope – an old man given a spontaneous kiss by a young nurse can still beam joy and pleasure. An old lady frail and feeble carefully makes a pot of tea to show that she can still manage in her own home....

Watching Judith Hann's report was indeed a mournful experience, and one can admire her for facing with such honesty the problems which we are all going to have to face in a big way sooner or later....

Ed. TT41

OBITUARY: VISCOUNT MONTGOMERY OF ALAMEIN

(Newsletter Old Comrades Association)

LEADER OF MEN

With the death of MONTGOMERY OF ALAMEIN, a chapter in the history of modern warfare is finally closed. The Monty legend began at Alamein. His decisive defeat of the brilliant and hitherto invincible Rommel – 'the Desert Fox' – marked a turn in the tides of war for Britain. As Churchill wrote later, before Alamein there were no victories, after Alamein there were no defeats. After Alamein, it was Tunis..Sicily..Normandy..the Rhine. These were the battle honours of the austere Monty, a man loved by his troops but who never drank or smoked, a General whose favourite books were said to be the Bible and Pilgrims Progress. Churchill described him as a 'Cromwellian figure – austere, severe, accomplished, tireless, his life given to the study of war…' Monty was a disciplinarian who disciplined no one more than himself. He was also a man who spoke with the firm conviction that he was right.

On May 4th, 1945 in a tent on windswept Luneburg Heath, five German plenipotentiaries stood in his presence and surrendered the German land, sea, and airforces in Northern Germany, Holland and Denmark. This was the supreme moment for a soldier who joined the army in 1908 – a man who knew war in all its aspects from the trenches of World War One to the exhilaration of command in a different conflict.

Ed. TT41

PERSONALITIES: LT. COLONEL SIR WILLIAM MOUNT. BART. DSO. TD

(Newsletter Old Comrades Association)

The 61st Reconnaissance Regiment was formed from the Brigade anti-tank companies supplemented by drafts of volunteers from the nine infantry Battalions. With his experience of mechanised troop movements, pre-war cross-country Recce and pursuit work, Sir William, then a Battery Commander in the Berkshire Yeomanry, was chosen to convert his body of individuals into a regiment, and to command it. Volunteers had expected to join a reasonably equipped unit: instead they found various infantry badges contemplating without enthusiasm the three-parts worn out 'Beaverettes' which looked most uninviting for a journey from point A to point B without incident. Yet in a few months, Sir William had created a spirit, and his insistence on super maintenance made our vehicles equal to the long journeys we were required to undertake during our training. He knew that success would depend on expert drivers and driver mechanics, so all other training was subordinated to the wishes of the Technical Adjutant. Also that Recce was of no value unless souls be returned, so those free from the Tech. Adjt's claws, found themselves with headphones screeching "Net again, net now". Three years later in France, the Regiment proved the value of his policies......Meanwhile, under Sir William's aspiration, the Regiment came to life as a Regiment. He would administer the most rasping 'rocket' yet was not slow to give credit when earned. His sense of humour was able to see the redeeming feature in most military crimes. When 'C' Squadron found the LMS wine cellar under the floorboards at the Station Café, and abstracted a number of bottles before being found out, he took the public, official view, but in private, he hailed it as 'C' Sqdn's first Recce role.

Behind the scenes, his influence on the development of the Recce Corps was tremendous, always thinking of improving organisation and equipment. He invented the system of mortar firing from the map, enabling mortar fire to hit the target with the first round instead of the plus and minus. An official similar type followed. He pressed for an Air OP as part of Recce outfit. This too received official blessing.

After much negotiation, Sir William succeeded in our transfer (at a record fee?) to the 50th (TT) Northumbrian Division at Brandon, and here we took up our Assault role with its waterproof and Landing Craft training etc. Our main D-Day role was to provide a skeleton assault Recce Regiment: under 8th Armoured Brigade. The plan was to break out of the bridgehead on the evening of D-Day and capture Villers Bocage on D + 1. The failure of the rhino ferries necessitated a modified plan on D + 2 although progress had been made on D and D1 days. However, after listening to the slow advancing of the tanks he rode forward in his carrier. Half an hour later his operator reported "My Sunray hit. Send Sunray Minor". He had been badly wounded in the thigh while standing up his full 6ft 1½ inches urging on the tanks. The military reward for all his work in forming, training and launching the Regiment into battle was the loss of his temporary rank after three months, but Sir William has much consolation in that to all who served under him he still remains 'the CO' of the Regiment.

GUARDIAN ANGEL

Not only did Gwynfryn Upward pull a paralysed Corporal Peter Harber out of the heat of battle in the 53rd Recce advance on the Dutch town of s'Hertogenbosch in 1944 but was also on hand 41 years later to catch him as he collapsed at a Cenotaph while honouring fallen colleagues.

A shell struck in a trench next to him, killing two of his men and wounding others. As he dashed from his own trench to help, another shell exploded and blew him 20 yards into a ditch, virtually buried and paralysed, and would have been a gonna but for a frantic pair of hands he felt clawing him from his grave. Only two came out of that action......and it was not until the Cenotaph ceremony of the 53rd Recce visit to s'Hertogenbosch 1985 that they met and recognised each other after ex-Corporal Peter Harber collapsed into the arms of Gwynfryn – twice he'd picked Peter from the floor – an incredible coincidence.

SMILE FOR THE CAMERA

One should never despair when dealing with anti-social individuals; most hardened criminals can be made to realise that crime does not pay – provided of course, that he is given time.

POET'S CORNER

JUST WHAT DOES IT MEAN?

Just what does it mean to wear a hat that looks neither this nor that,
Call it a cap or what you may, its come to the army and here to stay.
Just what does it mean to see that spear, that looks like lightning but never fear
Well to the fore, and swift as a ray, its come to the army and here to stay.
Just what does it mean to see these toughs, real army men without collar or cuffs.
"We belong to the Recce's" – You'll hear them say,
It's come to the army and here to stay.
Strong as lions and tough as steel, picked from an Empire where men are real.
Let not the blouse or cissy hat, mistake you from thinking other than that.
We're proud of our name, and emblems too, would you like to know just what we do?
Only the toughest can stand our training, summer winter snowing or raining,
On the march we step as one; "Come on my lads, there's a job to be done."
The Recce's are out, training without fear, they'll adjust their hat and straighten that spear,
Square their shoulders and glance to the rear –
Where the balance of the army is – get the idea?
On we push – we must get through, we've told you before, we've a job to do.
Recce's we're born and Recce's we'll die,
The cream of the service – our limits the sky.
Nineteen letters spell out a name
Standing for smartness, bravery and fame.
When you see them, well to the fore
It'll be us my lads, the RECONNAISSANCE CORPS.

A Gammack
Belgium 1945
61 Recce & 52 Recce:

(Wipe your eyes, lads. No wonder they gave us adjustable berets!) TT41

149

THE ORIGIN OF THE RECCE CORPS

One day 'Old Nick' sat dreaming
Surrounded by his crew.
He was plotting, planning, scheming,
Of mischief still to do.
When suddenly an imp of hell
Jumped up from the floor
And shouted out in accents loud
"Why not a Recce Corps?"

"You know our good friend Adolf
Has lent a helping hand
He's got the nations up in arms
Throughout the blinking land.
He's done his best to make things hot
For quite two years or more.
It's up to us to do our bit,
Why not a Recce Corps?"

The devil leapt from off his throne
With a wild satanic yell.
He grabbed the imp around the waist
And danced him all round hell.
"Good imp you've solved the problem
For when things start to bore
For raising plain or fancy hell
Why not a Recce Corps?"

I'll see the Army Council
And have them make a start.
We've done our best for them
So now they'll have to play their part.
Of course it won't be very hard
For there we've friends galore
Who'll only be too pleased I'm sure
To start a Recce Corps.

We'll rake in all the odds and sods
From every blinking batt
KOSB ies, Rifles, Royal Scots
And other mobs like that.
And don't forget our good old friends
Who served us well before.
Grab all the H.L.I. you can
To start the Recce Corps.

I'll leave it to you, you imps of hell
To pick the rank and file
For well you know the sort of troops
To suit our fiendish style.
You'll also pick the NCO's
But he ended with a roar
"I'll pick the bloody officers
To form the Recce Corps."

Then wide they opened up hell's gates
And out the imps did flee
And pounced on unsuspecting Jocks
And blokes like you and me.
They grabbed them from detention's gates
And off the taproom floor.
They slammed them all together
And they formed the Recce Corps.

From – Captain Johnnie Maxwell
52nd (Lowland) Recce Regt:

THE BEGINNING OF THE END

The clouds were low and overcast
The Invasion had begun at last,
The shores of France were just a haze,
Our Navy's guns were all ablaze.
The sea was angry, the waves did roar,
As they rolled our boats onto the shore.
The comradeship in those days was grand,
It enabled us to make a stand,
The Navy, the Army, the Airforce combined,
All pulling together with one thought in mind.
Tanks were burning a flaming red,
Inside their steel cases their crews were dead,
They shared their glory, they shared their sorrow,
They shared today, they shared tomorrow.
Let's nor forget those heroic men,
Who fought the 'BEGINNING OF THE END'.

John Brookes
(13th/18th Royal Hussars.)
9th June, 1944

John Brookes was a tank driver whose engine was flooded as he drove his tank down the ramp of the Tank Landing Craft into the sea blocking the exit for the rest. He (John) had to get out and dive under the water with a chain so that they could be pulled up the beach. It took three attempts at diving under and he was a non-swimmer. He wrote this poem the next day.

'WAR ECHOES OVER THIRTY YEARS'

Written by - Major Frank Harding, MC, OC 'B' Sqdn 61st Recce Regt
Published by – Arthur H Stockwell Ltd, Ilfracombe, Devon

EXERCISE SPARTAN (Feb/March, 1943)

As time went on invasionless, the cry
To reproduce war's likeness more was heard:
Make things unpleasant, toughen up the herd,
Put ginger in the Staff with moves by night.

So forth we went and back, to left and right,
From Hungerford northwards to Rickmansworth;
Dug trenches – with some joy – over Woburn,
Had lats. And showers in icy cold outside.

The Scheme concluded – downgraded our Div –
We heard the appreciation* from G** Brig.
In service dress and polished boots, no need
To dream of War tests. Captain gratefully
Recalled where by the Mess, at 'home' party,
He'd left his suit, undressed outdoors to sleep!

* Appreciation was the army term for summing up, not excluding much criticism.
** G – was the Command Staff operation and planning section.

IN MEMORIAM – WAR INTERVENED

War intervened, and thrust manhood on them,
Called them to arms when youth was freshly green.

War intervened and took their golden years:
Left us behind to mourn for friends in dream.

Are they now free whilst we are ageing here?
They keep for aye Youth, their Divinity!

'WAR ECHOES OVER THIRTY YEARS'

ON THE EVE

The lanes and fields of Anglia unfold
On maps read speedily in armoured cars,
By village clock of Brooke where bridge stays fast,
By meadow corner where the cowslips grow.

Then down to southern coast for night patrols
Where place names such as Hythe, Dymchurch are passed
To Sandgate and return, to where those last
Old sentries of Martello towers behold

The ever-shifting sea, now soon to bear
Armada on the ebb of Hitler's tide.
Then are the hosts in canvas camp confined,
Some in a wood called Nightingale: but where
No bird sings to the restless men at night,
Who fancy seeing ravens in the sky.

(In old English poetry, ravens presaged, and followed, battle and slaughter).

NEW REGIMENT 1941

'The Recce want you, and you're off tonight'
Said kindly adjutant, plunged somewhat in gloom.
One used to role in infantry, who liked
His men and colleagues, acted 'Turk'. But soon
The changes to ARCS, Bren Carriers, and new life
Of seek and hold, patrol and harbour, groom
The AFVs in Stables brought delight
To those selected for the Div's new pride.

Old discipline there was, with RSM
As fierce as any; self-reliance, brains
Too were encouraged, interest in lots
Of novel tactics, flanking, ranging. Friends
Were Gunners, Field and Anti-Tank; our aim
Of trusted information stemmed from top.

SEIZE AND HOLD

INVASION – 6TH JUNE 1944

'Twas on a rhino ferry
Coming over
We fired our rifles first –
To sudden laughter.

On Yankee ship we'd watched
How negro gunner,
Had fired with rolling eyes
At single Dornier.

Now we're set loose on raft
See, powerless,
Our bark towards the mines
Drift, engineless.

'Pot that, right centre, look!'
'One's over there!'
'Hurry, they're bastard duds,
We'll soon be clear!'

What hollow, false relief
To hug French shore:
And seek out mates – some lost
For evermore!

DESTINATION BERLIN

Monty stood up in his jeep:
'I'm not here to make flesh creep,
I intend to win the day
When I launch you in the fray.'

Monty stood up on the shore,
Spurred his troops on even more;
'Peg and peg your claim to ground,
Master-plan of mine is sound.'

Monty stood up on the Seine,
Looking back beyond the plain
To the shambles of Falaise,
And the West-front Nazi's grave.

Monty stood up in his car,
Having espied from afar
'Chutes in trees and gliders wrecked,
Atnkem: he gave cigarettes.

Monty stood up on the Rhine
The forest mud now left behind
And Holland floods: 'Thrust to the North
Deny the Russians Baltic ports!'

Monty stood upon the heath
On morrow of German defeat;
Saw the ghosts of general staff,
And like Macbeth raised no laugh.

Monty sat down in Berlin,
Eschewed Vodka, wine and gin;
Greeted Russians with delight,
Wondered who had won the fight?

CONCLUSION

Also from Frank Harding

1060 BOYS

Two young midland county boys, by name
Ansell and Humphries, stood for many more
Born about nineteen twenty-four,
Eager new intake, whence their army name.
One, widow's son, slender, reserved and grave,
Shirked not to speed his car through seas to shore;
One fresh-faced, jovial, duties lightly bore,
From carrier gunner, Corporal soon became.
One shattered by a mortar, took his pain
Like Moore, or Wolfe; one crushed in ambush, freed
His mates, and lay his agony to earth.
Their comrades thus steeled by their death, became
The sterner men: those who now live believe
No generation better proved its worth.

(These lines reflect the feelings of many of us about the 1060 'intake'.)

(Just a few of many memories recalled in verse by Frank Harding.)

Death only this mysterious truth unfolds,
The mighty soul how small a body holds.

Dryden

MONTGOMERY OF ALEMAIN

Character: - Montgomery, Bernard Law.

Born in Northern Ireland, November 1887.

Formative years spent in Tasmania where his father was a Bishop.

Returned to England to school, where he displayed team spirit only when he himself was the Captain.

Vain, self-centred, troublesome as a General.

At Sandhurst Royal Military College he was a bully. Was the ringleader of a gang who set fire to a cadet, for which he was reduced to the rank of cadet as a punishment.

He did have personal courage, winning the DSO in a bayonet charge as a subaltern during the 1st Battle of Ypres (World War 1).

He was also mean. He once leased military property to a fairground owner to raise money for Garrison amenities. In response to an appeal for a cancer hospital, he sent a cheque for £25.00 drawn on the 'Army Comfort Fund'. On another occasion he sent a youth organisation a cheque drawn on the '8th Army Benevolent Fund'.

In 1927 he married a Betty Carver – widow of an exceedingly rich officer killed at Gallipolli.

On the 12th June 1944, he sent a letter to his Chief of Staff in England in which he referred to the Air Marshal Leigh Mallory as 'a gutter bugger'.

SMILE FOR THE CAMERA

The RSM pulled up on his motorbike at the Squadron Fitters Workshop. "There's something wrong with my bike, fix it" he barked.

The fitter looked and said "There's a short circuit in the ignition".

RSM " Well, lengthen it and let me get going".

INCIDENTAL NOTES

On 24th June, 1944 the 43rd Reconnaissance Regiment, on board Landing Ship MT 41, 'The Derry Cundy', struck a mine off the beaches at 7 am with the loss of 330 men out of 500.

United States Court Martials
In all, 454 GI's were sentenced to death, of which 70 were actually executed. (Chiefly for rape and looting).

United States Air Force
During summer 1944, several hundred US Pilots, their courage abraded by the horrific odds against their survival, had set down their aircraft in Switzerland or Sweden and had been interned.

Combat Fatigue (Known as shell shock in World War 1)
One Field Hospital contained mostly wounds which were self-inflicted. During World War 1, an infantryman could count on being pulled out of the front-line for a rest period every two weeks. In World War 2, there had been no respite from action!

First British Airborne Division in Sicily
The American transport pilots had dropped the British troops, including their General, into the Mediterranean Sea several miles off the coast at the first sign of enemy flak!

Approx. 2000 British women were killed, wounded, or taken prisoner in World War 2, in all of the three services. Five girls won the Military Medal for bravery.

RECONNAISSANCE CORPS
STAINED GLASS WINDOW – ALL HALLOWS

(By the Tower, Byward Street, London EC 3.)

On Sunday 30th April 1950 at a memorial service in St Martin-in-the-Fields, London, a Table bearing the Corps Badge and a Book of Remembrance containing the Corps Roll of Honour were dedicated and later entrusted to the Revd P.B. (Tubby) Clayton MC by General Sir Bernard Paget, Colonel-Commandant of the Corps, to remain permanently in the Baptistery of the Church of All Hallows by the Tower, Guild Church of Toc H. On Remembrance Sunday 10 November 1985 a stained-glass window bearing the Corps Badge was dedicated at All Hallows. Annually, each Remembrance Sunday afternoon a service for fallen of the Corps is held at All Hallows. Wreaths are laid in the Baptistery by representatives of each Regiment

All Hallows-by-the-Tower Church is full of history, dating back to 400 years ago. First built by the Saxons over a Roman Villa, the floor of which may still be seen. Kings and Queens of earliest times worshipped here and much of the ground was the resting-place of many famous victims of the block.

Another interesting Memorial is the Field of Remembrance, St Mary's Churchyard, Westminster Abbey, where all regiments of the British Army are represented by a small plot. Doc Jarvis visited this scene on 11th November and in the Reconnaissance Section found a tribute to Captain Snook (A Sqdn). Who laid the Tribute was not indicated.

RECONNAISSANCE CORPS TOTAL CASUALTIES IN WORLD WAR TWO

The Reconnaissance Corps was not formed until January 1941, and was disbanded in August 1946. During this period approximately 20,000 men served within the ranks. Of this number over 10% gave their lives – 146 Officers and 1,961 other ranks. Another 30% were wounded on active service.

Their graves lie in 27 countries of the world, which are listed by The Commonwealth War Graves Commission Registers as follows –

AUSTRIA
ALGERIA
BELGIUM
BURMA
BORNEO
EGYPT
FRANCE
GERMANY
GHANA
HOLLAND
HONG KONG
ITALY
IRAQ
INDIA
JAPAN
LEBANON
LIBYA
MALAYA
PAKISTAN
SICILY
SOUTH AFRICA
SIAM
TUNISIA
UNITED KINGDOM – ENGLAND, SCOTLAND, & WALES.
UGANDA

Those whose graves lie within the UK consist mainly of those who were returned to hospital and who died of wound injuries later.

Roy Howard

RECONNAISSANCE CORPS WAR GRAVES
(N.W. EUROPEAN THEATRE)

NORMANDY

BANNEVILLE La CAMPAGNE.	Calvados	35	Recce	Casualties
BAYEUX CEMETERY	"	72	"	"
BROUAY CEMETERY	"	5	"	"
FONTENAY LE PESNEL	"	7	"	"
HERMANVILLE	"	8	"	"
HOTTOT-Les-BAGUES	"	7	"	"
LA DELIVRANDE	"	9	"	"
St. CHARLES DE PERCY	"	25	"	"
St. DESIR	"	10	"	"
St. MANVIEU CHEUX	"	7	"	"
RANVILLE	"	21	"	"
RYES	"	3	"	"
SEQUEVILLE-EN-BESSIN	"	2	"	"
TILLY-SUR-SEULLES	"	8	"	"

THE BAYEUX WAR MEMORIAL

*LISTS THE NAMES OF 176 MEMBERS OF THE RECONNAISSANCE CORPS
WHO HAVE NO KNOWN GRAVES.*

61ST RECONNAISSANCE REGIMENT
ROLL OF HONOUR

NAME	NUMBER	RANK	DATE OF DEATH
ABBEY, Thomas W.	5248541	Sgt.	23/06/1944
ALEXANDER, Stanley G	88303	Major	24/09/1944
ANDREWS, Albert T.	5245619	Sgt.	12/08/1942
ANSELL, Henry E.G.	5885250	Tpr.	11/08/1944
ASHTON, Squire	5890124	Cpl.	26/06/1944
BARNETT, Arthur R.	7674856	Cpl.	01/09/1944
BATER, Horace E.	6352017	Cpl.	03/08/1944
BLACK, Robert.	1500623	Cpl.	07/06/1944
BRANCH, Ernest H.	5386529	Tpr.	06/09/1944
BUCHAN, John H.	14297251	Tpr	02/09/1944
CARPENTER, Leslie E.	5384741	Sgt.	10/06/1944
CARTER, Dennis R.	14646512	Tpr.	30/12/1944
CHECKER, Dennis S.	5184059	Tpr.	01/12/1942
CLAY, William J.	5253520	Tpr.	15/10/1944
COLE, Arthur J.	5629938	Tpr	20/06/1944
COLLIER, Alan J.	10600855	Tpr	12/07/1945
COLLIER, Joseph.	10602535	Tpr.	15/06/1944
COLLINGWOOD, Richard C.	5187667	Tpr.	30/12/1944
COOPER, Harry.	7927245	Cpl.	19/06/1944
COTTERELL, Hugh R.	203314	Lt.	26/07/1943
DAY, John	5181510	Tpr	02/09/1944
DOCHERTY, Matthew.	5256990	Tpr.	20/06/1944
DUNNINGTON, Joseph A.	4800261	Sgt.	05/08/1944
DYMOND, Leslie D.W.	5339820	Tpr.	07/06/1944
EDWARDS, Stanley T.	5384009	Sgt.	04/01/1945
EKINS, Kenneth R.	5884365	Sgt.	20/06/1944
ELL, Robert G.	328238	L/Sgt.	03/08/1944
GRIFFITHS, William A.	5114831	Sgt.	15/06/1944
HARPER, Edward.	5380505	Sgt.	19/10/1944
HALLETT, W.J.	5341957	Tpr.	24/03/1943
HEATON, William H.	5120826	Tpr.	03/08/1944
HAYNES, N.	Unknown.	Tpr.	Unknown.
HUMPHREYS, Eric R.	10602515	Cpl.	19/06/1944
KERSHAW, Frank.	10602574	Tpr.	20/06/1944
MACKINTOSH, Douglas.	6348177	Cpl.	31/12/1944
MATTHEWS, Albert E.	5676900	Tpr.	09/09/1944

McHUGH, Ronald.	10602576	Tpr.	15/06/1944
METCALFE, Gerald T.	10602579	Cpl.	04/01/1945
MOSS, William R.	5385691	Sgt.	06/06/1944
NEWELL, Arthur H.	6352355	Tpr.	06/06/1944
RAINE, Maurice.	14544569	Tpr.	11/10/1944
RAINFORD, Richard H.	14546131	Tpr.	06/06/1944
RICKWOOD, James J.	2563185	Sgt.	12/08/1944
ROBINSON, Reginald.	5387636	Tpr.	11/09/1944
ROWBOTHAM, John.	10602528	Tpr.	22/02/1945
RUANE, Thomas.	3248648	Sgt.	10/06/1944
SHAW,	Unknown	Cpl.	11/12/1941
SLATER, John T.	10602553	Tpr.	20/07/1944
SMITH, Frederick S.R.	7016258	Tpr.	03/11/1944
SMITH, Harold.	5884676	Tpr.	18/08/1943
SMITH, Sidney	5337851	L/Sgt.	09/09/1944
SNOOK, Herbert S.	229268	Capt.	21/04/1945
STAMP, Stanley.	14245541	Tpr.	10/09/1944
STEVENS, Robert G.	6354781	Tpr.	03/08/1944
STEVENSON, William J.	10602554	Tpr.	05/08/1944
STEWARD, J.W.	4544055	Tpr.	04/01/1945
TOOTELL, John.	10602586	Tpr.	18/07/1944
TURNER, Charles E.	5254309	Tpr.	17/07/1944
VEATER, W.	14323375	Cpl.	22/02/1945
WADE, Arnold.	4625404	Tpr.	26/06/1944
WALLACE, Cecil A.	3196260	Sgt.	19/06/1944
WALL, F.	5388128	Tpr.	10/11/1941
WEBB, John.	14277079	Tpr.	15/06/1944
WEBB, Thomas.	14561565	Tpr.	30/12/1944
WHITEHOUSE, Roy G.	5050415	Cpl.	10/10/1944
WILLIAMS, Gwilyam J.	5253854	Tpr.	26/06/1944
WOODCOCK, Reginald.	5250716	L/Cpl.	24/03/1943
YOUNG, Alexander.	3056568	Sgt.	04/01/1945

MISSING WITHOUT TRACE

FLETCHER, G.H.	14509529	Tpr.
JARVEN, W.	14575563	Tpr.
LATTER, H.	14242007	Tpr.
ORTON, W.	5110993	Tpr.
STANNEY, J.F.	106002530	Cpl.
TANNER, L. E.	14638920	Tpr.
WATT, J.A.	7933936	Tpr.